EXPANDED SECOND EDITION

The DEAD TOWNS of SUNBURY, GA. and DORCHESTER, S. C.

By *Paul McIlvaine*

Copyright 1971 by Paul M. McIlvaine
All Rights Reserved

Second Edition Published 1975

International Standard Book Number 0-9600410-2-8
Library of Congress Catalog Card Number: 71-156742
Manufactured in the United States of America

Published by Paul M McIlvaine
Route 3, Box 90, Hendersonville, N. C. 28739
Phone 704-692-3971

*Printed by Groves Printing Co.
Asheville, N. C. 28802*

BIBLIOGRAPHY

The following organizations recommended and supplied historical material: Georgia Historical Society, Savannah; South Carolina Historical Society, Charleston; Historic Preservation Section, Georgia Department of Natural Resources, Atlanta; Georgia Department of Archives, Atlanta; Midway Museum, Midway, Georgia; National Archives and Records Service, Washington, D. C.; Library of Congress, Washington, D. C.; The United Society for the Propagation of the Gospel in Foreign Parts, London, England. The following sources contributed to this volume:

The Dead Towns of Georgia, by C. C. Jones, 1878
Revolutionary Records of Georgia, Volume II
The American Revolution in Georgia, 1763-1789, by Kenneth Coleman
Colonial Georgia, by Trevor Reese
McCall's History of Georgia, 1816
Steven's History of Georgia, 1859
White's Historical Collections of Georgia, 1855
Travels through North and South Carolina and Georgia &c, by William Bartramm, 1792
Button Gwinnett, by C. F. Jenkins, 1926
History and Records of Midway Church, James Stacy, 1903
Midway Congregational Church — A Paragon — 1630 — 1751 — 1929, by H. B. Folsom
Midway Church Record Book at Midway Museum
Georgia Mineral Newsletter, Volume VIII, No. 3, Autumn 1955
Liberty County Herald, Special Museum — Historical Edition, November 26, 1959
South Carolina Historical and Genealogical Magazine, 1905
Harper's New Monthly Magazine, December 1875

ILLUSTRATIONS

Photographs on pages 32, 33, 39, 54, 61, 64, 66, 78, 80 were taken by author in 1968

Page 4 1818 map section of Georgia, Library of Congress
Page 12 Town Plan of Sunbury, drawn by author from material found in "The Dead Towns of Georgia"
Page 13 Aerial photo of Sunbury, Soil Conservation Service, 1953
Page 22 Sunbury home, drawn by author from material supplied by the Midway Museum.
Page 31 Layout of Fort Morris, drawn by author from information found in "The Dead Towns of Georgia".
Page 34 1780 map of Sunbury, section redrawn from "Sketch of the Northern Frontiers of Georgia," Library of Congress
Page 59 Map of Old Sunbury Road, Georgia Geological Survey.
Page 69 1775 map section of Charleston area, Library of Congress.
Page 72 Town Plan of Dorchester, redrawn by author from 1742 map in "History and Records of Midway Church."
Page 76 The White Meeting House, drawn by the author from a sketch in Harpers New Monthly Magazine, December 1875
Page 81 Layout of Fort Dorchester, drawn by author from sketch in "South Carolina Historical and Genealogical Magazine," May 1905

CONTENTS

SUNBURY, GEORGIA

	PAGE
THE DEAD TOWN OF SUNBURY	5
THE MIDWAY SETTLEMENT	8
THE FOUNDING OF SUNBURY	11
GEORGIA'S ECONOMY	17
SUNBURY CHURCHES	19
THE AMERICAN REVOLUTION	25
GEORGIA PREPARES FOR WAR	30
BRITISH OCCUPATION OF GEORGIA	41
POST WAR SUNBURY	53
POSTAL SERVICE	57
THE SUNBURY ROAD	58
SUNBURY SLEEPS	67

DORCHESTER, SOUTH CAROLINA

THE DEAD TOWN OF DORCHESTER	69
THE DORCHESTER FREE SCHOOL	74
THE WHITE MEETING HOUSE	76
ST. GEORGE'S ANGLICAN CHURCH	78
FORT DORCHESTER	79
THE REVOLUTIONARY WAR	80
POSTAL SERVICE	82
DORCHESTER SLUMBERS	82

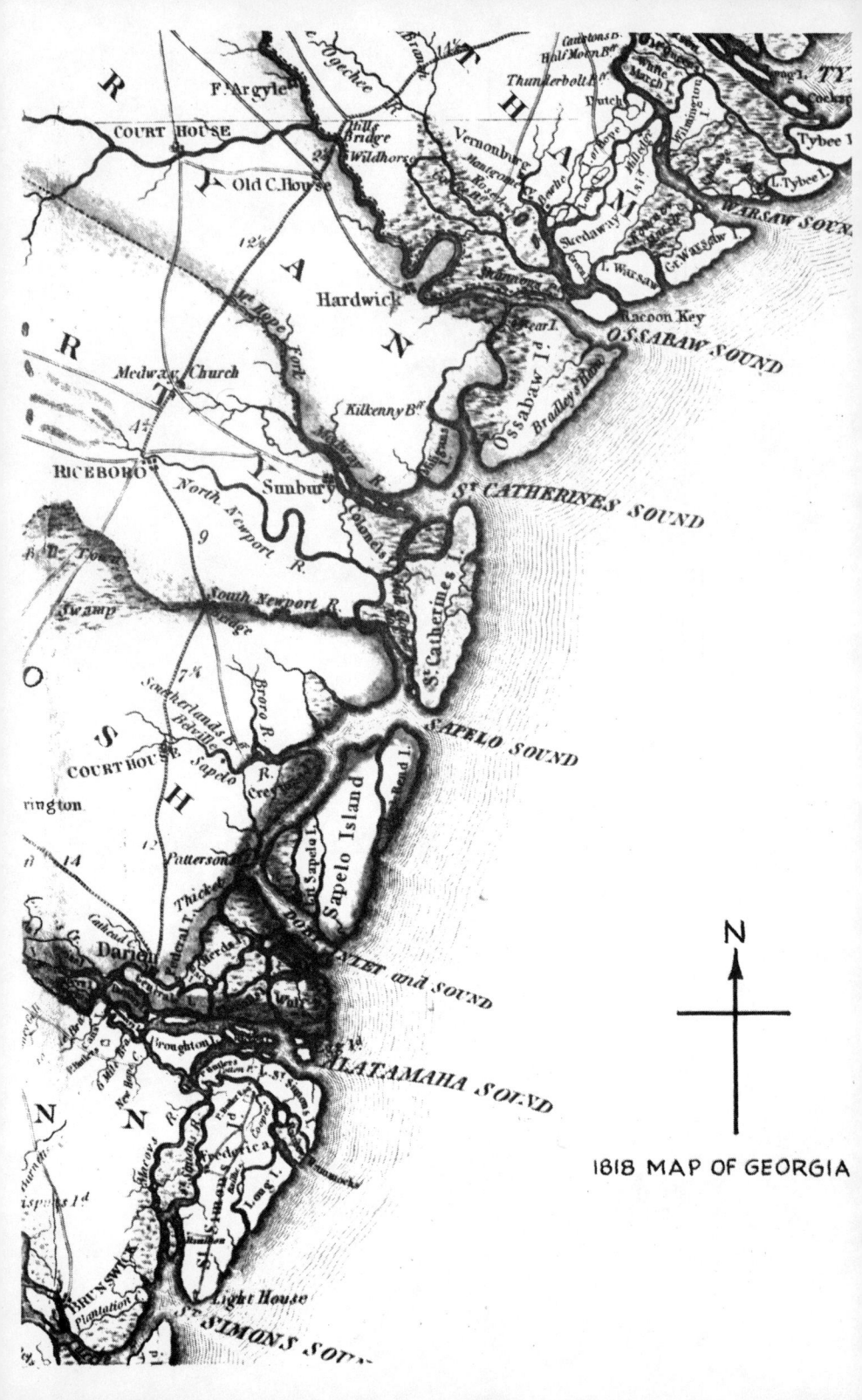

1818 MAP OF GEORGIA

THE DEAD TOWN OF SUNBURY

This is the story of the dead Colonial town of Sunbury, Georgia — a town that probably produced more famous people per square foot of real estate than any other town in America. In Revolutionary times, Sunbury was said to have rivalled Savannah as a commerical seaport, but, today not a single original building is left standing, and the old town site lies sleeping on the bank of the Midway River, 28 miles below Savannah. Only the old Colonial cemetery and the ruins of Ft. Morris, now undergoing restoration, are left to mark the scene of its demise.

How the story of Sunbury has evaded the American history books is a mystery, since it obviously played a very important role in the founding of our Nation. Three signers of the Declaration of Independence were connected with it in one way or another. Lyman Hall owned a home there, Button Gwinnett owned a home on the offshore island of St. Cathrine's, and George Walton, the third Georgia signer, was held prisoner there by the British, who captured the town in 1779 and held it until 1783.

Sunbury was founded by the descendants of a migrating colony of Puritans who originally landed at Mattapan on the Neponset River in Massachusetts and founded the town of Dorchester in 1630. Five years later, in 1635, over half of this nomad group moved in a body to Windsor, Connecticut. In 1696, a group of descendants from the Puritan colony at Dorchester, Massachusetts, joined by others from neighboring towns, migrated to South Carolina where they founded the town of Dorchester, 18 miles above Charleston. In 1752, the Puritan colonists of Dorchester moved in a body to Midway, Georgia. In 1758 these colonists established the seaport town of Sunbury, eleven miles east, on the Midway River.

Here is a partial list of the great people, and the ancestors of great people, who came from Sunbury and the Midway District. In addition to the signers of the Declaration of Independence, mentioned above, Sunbury produced three United States Senators, John Elliot, Alfred Cuthbert and Augustus O. Bacon. One U. S. Representative, John A. Cuthbert. The first United States Minister to China and Japan, John Elliot Ward.

Four Georgia Governors called it home. They were Nathan Brownson, Richard Howley, John Martin and Lyman Hall.

5

Button Gwinnett served as "President of the State of Georgia" for two months after the sudden death of Governor Archibald Bulloch in March 1777.

Three ministers of the Midway Church were ancestors of famous people. Reverend Abiel Holmes was the father of Oliver Wendell Holmes, the author, and the grandfather of Oliver Wendell Holmes, the United States Supreme Court Chief Justice. Reverend Jedidiah Morse was the father of S.F.B. Morse, the inventor of the telegraph. Reverend I.S.K. Axson was the grandfather of the first Mrs. Woodrow Wilson. General Daniel Stewart was the great grandfather of President Theordore Roosevelt. Dr. Francis Goulding was the author of "The Young Marooners," and the inventor of the lock-stitch sewing machine. Unfortunately, he failed to patent it.

Dr. Louis LeConte botanist and owner of the Le Conte Botanical Gardens on his plantation, "Woodmanston," produced the famous Le Conte pear tree which was used to stock pear orchards throughout the South. So famous were his Gardens that visitors were attracted from many foreign countries. Dr. Le Conte was the father of two scientist sons, John and Joseph. John Le Conte was the first president of the University of California.

For the purpose of this manuscript, Midway and Sunbury have been combined since the two places were so closely associated. For instance, Lyman Hall owned homes at both Sunbury and Midway. Reverend Abiel Holmes was the minister of the Midway Church and was an instructor at the Sunbury Academy. John Martin, Naval Officer at the Port of Sunbury was on the board of selectmen of the Midway Church and of the Society.

To better understand the birth of Sunbury in 1758, an over all look at the founding of Georgia, the thirteenth original colony, is helpful for background. The foundations of Georgia were laid in a British Royal Charter in 1732 which set its boundaries as follows:

"All those lands, countries and territories situate, lying and being in part of South Carolina in America which lies from the most southern stream of river there, commonly called Savannah, all along the sea coast to the southward unto the most southern stream of a certain other great water or river called the Altamaha, and westerly from the heads of the said rivers respectively in direct lines to the South Seas; and all that share, circuit and precinct of land within the said boundaries, with the islands on the sea lying opposite to the eastern coast of the said lands, within twenty leagues of the same, which are not inhabited already or settled by any authority derived from the Crown of Great Britain."

From this description it can be seen that England did not consider Georgia to have any westward land boundary. Early maps show Georgia extending to the Mississippi River.

In order to begin colonization, a corporation was established in London under the name of the "Trustees for Establishing the Colony of Georgia in America." Its authority was to legislate the Colony's government for a period of 21 years, at the end of which time the grant was to revert to the Crown.

James Edward Oglethorpe was selected by the Trustees to lead the first immigration to Georgia, and a two-hundred ton frigate carrying the first group of 114 carefully selected immigrants set sail from England, November 17, 1732. They reached America in January 1733, and after sailing up the Savannah River some fifteen miles, selected a sandy pine-covered bluff, and here built the town of Savannah.

By 1737, five towns and a number of small villages had been erected. Savannah now had 140 houses and was prospering. Augusta, further inland, was growing on Indian trade. Frederica, on St. Simon's Island, and Darien on the Altamaha were being settled. Ebenezer was being built by a colony of German Salzburgers.

Life in Georgia was not easy. These early settlements were small, primitive, and life was precarious. A stern living had to be wrestled from the ground with primitive tools. To the South, the Spaniards in Florida were menacing, and all about them a hostile Indian population had to be reconciled.

In a closing account of its accomplishments during its charter period of government, the Trustees in 1751, reported to Parliament that with grants of 130,000 pounds, large numbers of British and foreign Protestants had been sent overseas, and that Georgia's population was estimated at 1,700 whites and 400 blacks. It stated that courts and local governments had been established, and that forts and many public works had been constructed.

In May 1752, the authority of the Trustees came to an end and Georgia duly became a royal province. Its government now took on the character of the other British colonies in America. The executive head of the government was a governor appointed by the Crown in England. Two houses made up the legislature. The Upper House of Assembly, actually the governor's council sitting for legislative business, and the Commons House of Assembly made up of elected residents of Georgia who owned at least fifty acres of land.

There were three main courts. A Court of Errors, the highest court which was made up of the Governor and his Council. A General Court which was a court of general jurisdiction, and several Peace Courts commonly called courts of conscience because decisions were said to have been made by conscience rather than legal training. In Sunbury, Button Gwinnett, one of the signers of the Declaration of Independence, sat on such a court as Justice of the Peace in 1767 and 1768.

The governor and other administrative officials were guided by detailed instructions from England. The more important executive officials such as the governor, the attorney general, the chief justice, the secretary, the receiver of general quit rents, the surveyor general, the provost marshal, and the custom officials were paid by a Georgia civil list provided by Parliament. Since many of these officials were sent from England, it was possible for the Crown to keep a close rein on the administration of the new colony.

It was at this juncture in Georgia history, 1752, that the first immigrants from the Puritan colony at Dorchester, South Carolina began arriving at Midway, Georgia—a movement that was to lead to the founding of Sunbury in 1758.

THE MIDWAY SETTLEMENT

In 1696, in response to a petition from Puritan plantation owners north of Charleston, a group of Dorchester, Massachusetts colonists were sent to South Carolina to establish a Congregationist Church. They settled on the Ashley River and named their town Dorchester. The group was lead by Reverend Joseph Lord, a Harvard graduate. At this time, the Church of England was dominant in South Carolina.

Dorchester was laid out as a market town. It contained 116 lots and had a town square and commons. Its strategic location on the Ashley River made it a shipping point and a trading center for the frontier. The surrounding land was low and swampy with many fertile hammocks. Rice was the chief money crop.

By 1752 it became necessary for the people of Dorchester to migrate again. For the sake of a compact community, they had selected only small tracts of land to farm, and these tracts now had lost much fertility. To compound the situation, when these tracts were divided among surviving children, they became too small to support their owners.

Accordingly, in May 1752, they sent three of their members to Midway, Georgia, and five others in June, to appraise that location as a possible site for resettlement. All were pleased at what they had found so they applied for a land grant in Savannah on their way home. On July 11, 1752 a grant of 22,500 acres was awarded to forty-four petitioners.

The following persons got 500 acres each: John Stevens, Sr., John Stevens, Jr., Benjamin Baker, Parmenas Way, James Way, Edward Way, Andrew Way, Joseph Way, Nathaniel Way, John Lupton, Samuel Stevens, Reverend John Osgood, Sarah Osgood, Richard Spencer, William Baker, Richard Baker, Richard Giradeau, Samuel Burnley, Joseph Bacon, Samuel Bacon, John Norman, Richard Woodcraft, John Mitchell, Sarah Mitchell, James Edwards, John Elliot, Barock Norman, John Stewart, Samuel Glass, Robert Echols, John Quarterman, David Russ, William Lupton, Joseph Oswald, Jacob Weston, Johnathan Bacon, Daniel Slade, John Winn, Edward Sumner, William Graves and Joseph Norman. 300 acres went to Joshua Clark, and 400 acres for the church glebe.

Twenty eight people recieved 9,650 additional acres in a second grant issued August 6, 1752. Those receiving 500 acres were John Graves, Isaac Bradwell, Elizabeth Simmons, Hugh Dowse, Peter Goulding, Daniel Duncan, Isaac Duncan, Palmer Goulding, Thomas Stevens, Jr., Joseph Massey, N. Bradwell and James Christie. 400 acres went to Elizabeth Baker, 300 acres to James Baker, William Chapman, and Rebecca Quarterman. 250 acres to Thomas Stevens, Joseph Stevens, and Joseph Bacon, Jr. 200 acres to John Churchill, John Wheeler, Joseph Winn, Moses Way, Daniel Cannon, John Shave, Joseph Baker and Thomas Way, Jr., and 100 acres to John Gordon.

The terms under which grants were originally made in Georgia provided that 500 acre tracts could be conveyed only to persons approved by the Trust, and that such persons should at their own expense, and within twelve months from date of grant, bring ten able-bodied men servants not younger than twenty years to settle upon the land. These grants could not be transferred without special approval by the Trust. However, this was amended in May, 1750 so that new grants could convey "an absolute inheritance to grantees, their heirs and assigns."

The first settlers to arrive from Dorchester were Mr. Benjamin Baker and family and Mr. Samuel Baker and family on December 6, 1752. The immigration reached its peak in the years 1754-55-56. According to the records of the Midway Church Society, now stored at the Midway Museum, thirty-nine families came from the Dorchester-Beach Hill area of South Carolina, four families from Pon-Pon and one from Charleston.

Preparations for the move began a year or two in advance. After harvesting their crops in the fall in Dorchester and Beach Hill, the planters with able-bodied hands, came to Midway during the winter where they cleared the land and built their houses. Early the following spring they brought their families, slaves and animals, and planted their crops, thus avoiding a cropless year. It was estimated that by 1771, when the migration came to an end, about 350 whites and 1,500 blacks had moved in.

It must be supposed that a number of settlers were already in the Midway district when the Dorchester congregation arrived. When the General Assembly convened in Savannah in 1751, the area was represented by Audley Maxwell, indicating that the population was large enough to warrant representation.

Just why these settlers located their houses amid the Midway swamps instead of choosing higher ground to the East or West can be rationalized only by their ignorance of the malaria menace, and their desire to be close to their rice crops which flourished in the swamps. At this time rice was the chief money crop of the local plantation owners.

These early settlers practiced the most primitive kind of agriculture. Ploughs were unknown and the ground was worked with hoes. Fencing rails had to be split by ax and carried on the heads of the Negroes. The rice was harvested and threshed by hand before being transported by wagon to market. Corn was planted on the high ground and each homestead maintained a truck garden, chickens, pigs and cows. The countryside was filled with game. The rice paddies were the habitat of wild geese and ducks. Turkeys and deer abounded. Nearby herds of buffalo grazed, and the swamps were filled with terrapins and fish.

At Midway, nature had been most generous in supplying every kind of living thing including great quantities of mosquitoes. The planters invariably built their homes at the edges of the swamps, and soon became victims of malaria, which was listed in their records as "bilious fever". Following attacks of "bilious fever" in the fall, the settlers became victims of "pleurisies" in the winter and died.

The first houses built were made of wood and were unlined on the inside. They were one story high, with dormer windows in the roof, heated by hearths built into clay chimneys. The consequences of malaria and pneumonia on the settlers living in these damp, cold, and drafty places was staggering. Records kept by the Midway Church Society listed 193 births and 134 deaths between the years of 1752 and 1772. Checking the epitaphs on the tombstones in the old Midway Cemetery, today, one is impressed by the numerous markers for infants, and the short life spans of the adults. The deaths of mothers, wives and husbands in their early twenties was the rule rather than the exception. It is surprising that the Negroes were immune to malaria and had a much better life expectancy than the whites.

THE FOUNDING OF SUNBURY

Thus were the unhealthy conditions existing in the Midway district when the planters began casting about for a more healthy place to move their homes and families, and for a seaport closer than Savannah through which to export the rice from their plantations.

Mark Carr, who had been granted 500 acres of land at the mouth of the Midway river, conveyed 300 acres, on June 20, 1758, to James Maxwell, Kenneth Baillie, John Elliot, Grey Elliot, and John Stevens with the stipulation that the land be used for a town site. One hundred acres were dedicated as a common, for the use of future inhabitants; —and in further trust—that they, the said James Maxwell, Kenneth Baillie, John Elliot, Grey Elliot, and John Stevens and their successors, should sell and dispose of all and singular the lots to be laid out in the said town of Sunbury and for the proper use and behoof of the said Mark Carr.

There were two theories on how the town of Sunbury and the river Midway got their names. One theory held that the town and river were named after a town and river in England by the same names. The river was spelled Medway. The other theory, that Sunbury was named for its sunny location on the

Plan for Town of SUNBURY, GA.

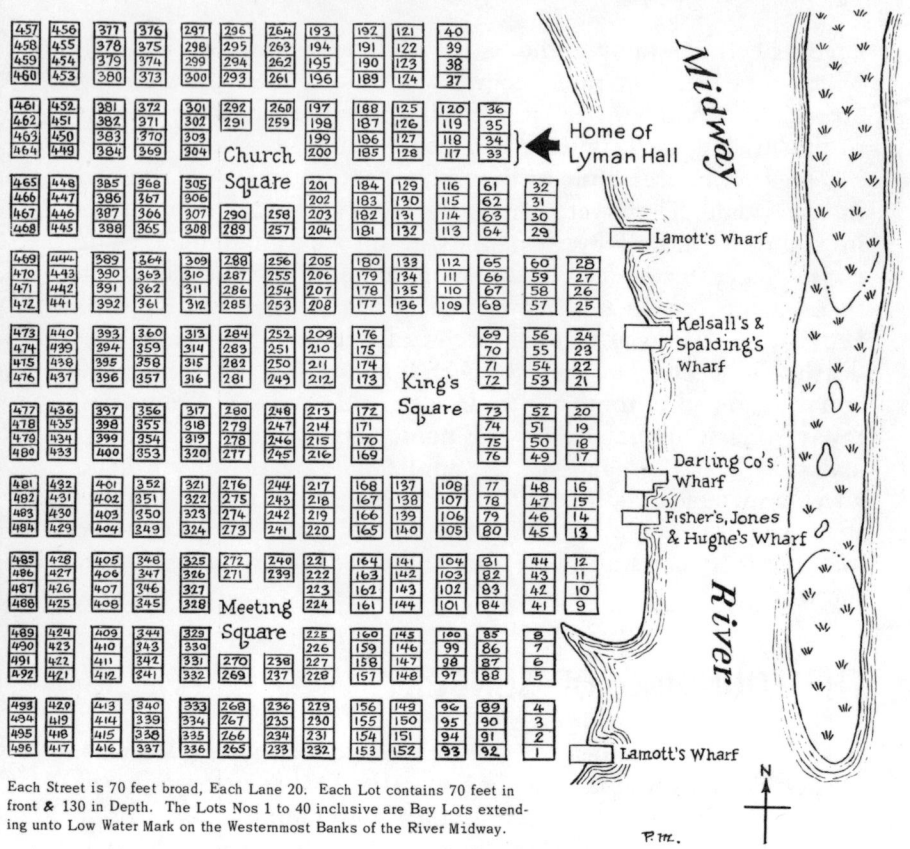

Each Street is 70 feet broad, Each Lane 20. Each Lot contains 70 feet in front & 130 in Depth. The Lots Nos 1 to 40 inclusive are Bay Lots extending unto Low Water Mark on the Westermost Banks of the River Midway.

banks of the river—Sunbury literally meaning sun town. And the Midway river was so named because of its half way location between Savannah and Darien.

Immediately upon conveyance of the 300 acres from Mark Carr, the five Trustees drew plans and began laying out the town. Sunbury had 496 lots and three squares called King's Square, Church Square and Meeting Square. The lots were uniform in size, each fronting 70 feet and running to a depth of 130 feet. There were four lots to the block, and each block was bounded on three sides by streets 75 feet wide, and on the fourth side by a lane 20 feet wide. Overall, the town was 3,430 feet north and south and east and west it measured 1,880 at the north boundary and 2,230 feet at the south boundary. This variation was caused by a bend in the Midway River.

Aerial photograph of the town site of Sunbury, today.

Within a short time settlers and merchants began arriving to build homes, stores and wharfs. Just how rapidly this occurred can be seen by a letter five years later in 1763 by Georgia's Governor, Sir James Wright to Lord Halifax in London.

"I judged it necessary for his Majecty's service that Sunbury—a well settled place, having an exceeding good harbour and inlet from the sea—should be made a Port of Entry and I have appointed Thomas Carr, Collector, John Martin, Naval Officer, for the same. There are eightly dwelling houses in the place, three considerable merchant stores supplying the town and planters in the neighborhood with all kinds of necessary goods; and around it for about fifteen miles is one of the best settled parts of the country."

In McCall's History of Georgia, printed in 1811, it is stated, "Soon after its settlement and organization as a town, it rose

13

into considerable commercial importance. Emigrants came from different quarters to this healthy maritime port, particularly from Bermuda; about seventy came from that island, but unfortunately for them and the reputation of the town, a mortal epidemic broke out and carried off about fifty of their number the first year; it is highly probable they brought the seeds of the disease with them. Of the remainder, as many as were able returned to their native country. This circumstance, however, did not very much retard the growing state of this eligible spot; a lucrative trade was carried on with the various parts of the West Indies in lumber, rice, indigo, corn, etc. Seven square rigged vessels have been known to enter the port of Sunbury in one day, and about the years 1769 and 1770 it was thought by many, in point of commercial importance to rival Savannah. In this prosperous state it continued with very little interruption until the war commenced between Great Britain and America."

On September 20, 1773, Governor James Wright, issued a report on the conditions of the Province of Georgia. In his report to London he stated that Savannah and Sunbury were the only two ports in the Province, and that in the previous year, 1772, fifty-six vessels of various sorts were entered and cleared the customs house in the port of Sunbury. He described the inlet leading to the town as very good and stated fifteen feet of water could be carried up to the town located twelve miles from the sea.

Also in Governor Wright's report were statistics that the population of Georgia had increased from 6,000 whites and 3,500 blacks in 1761 to 18,000 whites and 15,000 Negroes in 1773. The centers of population were located between the Savannah and the Altahama Rivers—Sunbury's location—the lower area between the Ogeechee and Savannah Rivers, and up the Savannah River to Augusta.

That Sunbury was sharing in this population expansion can be seen from the fact that 317 of the lots within the town had been sold by about 1775.[1]

Lot[2] Owner

1	Mark Carr	4	Grey Elliott	7	Francis Arthur
2	Arthur Carnaby	5	Francis Arthur	8	John Cubbage
3	Grey Elliott	6	William Graves	9	James Maxwell

Notes: [1] The Dead Towns of Georgia 1878
[2] Unsold lots not listed

Lot	Owner				
10	Mary Spry	65	John Lawson	119	John Elliot
11	Samuel Bennerworth	66	John Lawson	120	John Elliot
12	Steven Dickinson	67	Thomas Ralph	121	Benjamin Stevens
13	James Fisher, Schmidt	68	John Quarterman, Sr.	122	John Lynn
14	& Molich	69	Thomas Goldsmith	123	John Lynn
15	Swinton & Co.	70	James Houstoun	125	John Sutherland
16	Darling & Monro	71	John Stevens	126	John Sutherland
17	Francis Arthur	72	Mark Carr	127	Samuel Jeanes
18	James Derwell	73	Hugh Clark	128	Samuel Jeanes
19	Swinton & Co.	74	Hugh Clark	129	Joseph Tickener
20	Thomas Peacock	75	Kenneth Baillie, Sr.	130	William Miller
21	Andrew Darling	76	Kenneth Baillie, Sr.	131	Richard Mills
22	Thomas Young	77	Paris Way	132	Richard Mills
23	Thomas Young	78	Nathaniel Yates	133	Peter McKay
24	Roger Kelsall	79	William Dunham	134	James Miller
25	John James	80	Charles West	135	James Miller
26	Joseph Bacon	81	Daniel Slade	136	David Jervey
27	John Stewart, Sr.	82	Jacob Lockerman	137	William David
28	John Lupton	83	Samuel West	138	William David
29	Dunbar, Young & Co.	84	Thomas Carter, P. Schmidt	139	Joseph Serjeant
30	Dunbar, Young & Co.	85	John Elliot	140	John Jones
31	John Elliott	86	John Elliot	141	Strong Ashmore
32	James Dunham	87	William Baker	142	Francis Arthur
33	Lyman Hall	88	William Baker	143	Donald McKay
34	Lyman Hall	89	Audley Maxwell	144	Donald McKay
35	Samuel Miller	90	Elizabeth Simmons	145	Andrew Way
36	Kenneth Baillie, Sr.	91	John Graves	146	James Fisher
37	Samuel Bennerworth	92	John Graves	147	George Monis
38	Samuel Bennerworth	93	Robert Bolton	148	Thomas Way
39	William Sererson	94	John Baker	149	James Hatcher
40	William Sererson	95	John Humphreys	150	James Hatcher
41	Mark Carr	96	James Fisher, Francis Guilland	151	Francis Arthur
42	Tabitha Bacon			152	Francis Arthur
43	Tabitha Bacon	97	John Lupton	153	Francis Arthur
44	John Winn	98	John Lupton	154	Francis Arthur
45	David Jervey	99	Henry Saltus	155	John Perkins
46	David Jervey	100	Donald McKay	156	John Perkins
47	Francis Arthur	101	Steven Dickinson	157	William Love
48	Francis Lee	102	Steven Dickinson	158	William Love
49	John Quarterman, Jr.	103	William Clark	159	Charles West, Schmit
50	James Dowell	104	Thomas Christie	160	& Molich
51	John Irvine	105	Samuel Jeanes	161	Charles West
52	Jeremiah Irvine	106	Moses Way	162	Charles West
53	Darling & Co.	107	William David	163	William Peacock
54	Matthew Smallwood	108	Paynter Dickenson	164	William Peacock
55	William Peacock	109	Francis Lee	165	Charles West
56	Isaac Lines	110	Francis Lee	166	Charles West
57	John Osgood	111	James Harley	167	William Davis
58	Rebecca Way	112	Samuel Bacon	168	William Davis
59	John Stewart, Sr.	113	Tabitha Bacon	169	Francis Lee
60	John Lupton	114	John Stewart, Sr.	170	Francis Lee
61	James Dunham	115	John Stewart, Sr.	171	Thomas Vincent
62	John Shave	116	John Stewart, Sr.	172	Benjamin Baker
63	Jacob Lockerman	117	Stephen Dickenson	173	Grey Elliott
64	Paynter Dickerson	118	Stephen Dickenson		

Lot	Owner				
174	Grey Elliott	237	John Milchett	314	Samuel Tomlinson
175	Grey Elliott	238	John Milchett	315	Samuel Tomlinson
176	Grey Elliott	239	James Andrew	317	William Swinton
177	John Lupton	240	James Andrew	318	William Swinton
178	John Lupton	241	William Dunham	319	William Swinton
179	John Lupton	242	William Dunham	320	William Swinton
180	John Lupton	243	Samuel Jeanes	340	Peter McKay
181	T. Quarterman	244	Winw'd McIntosh	341	Peter McKay
182	Joseph Bacon	245	David Jervey	342	Peter McKay
185	Susannah Jones	246	David Jervey	343	Peter McKay
186	Susannah Jones	247	Francis Lee	344	Peter McKay
189	Barnard Romans	248	Samuel Morecock	345	Peter McKay
190	Barnard Romans	249	Mark Carr	346	Peter McKay
191	Barnard Romans	250	Mark Carr	347	Peter McKay
192	Barnard Romans	251	George Bodington	348	Peter McKay
200	John K. Zubley	252	Mary Bateman	349	Peter McKay
205	Edward Way	253	John Goff	350	Peter McKay
206	Edward Way	257	Robert Bolton	351	Peter McKay
207	James Fisher	258	Robert Bolton	352	Thomas Quarterman
208	James Fisher	265	Mark Carr	353	Barrack Norman
209	Edward Maham	266	Mark Carr	354	Barrack Norman
210	Edward Maham	267	John Bryan	355	Barrack Norman
211	Richard Spencer	268	John Bryan	356	Tarah, Sr.
212	Richard Spencer	269	Patrick McKay	357	Francis Arthur
213	William Swinton	270	Patrick McKay	358	Francis Arthur
214	William Swinton	271	Benjamin Andrew	359	Frederick Hobrendorff
215	William Swinton	272	Benjamin Andrew	360	Frederick Hobrendorff
216	William Swinton	273	Morgan Tabb	361	Joseph Richardson
217	Samuel Jeanes	274	Morgan Tabb	362	Joseph Richardson
218	Samuel Jeanes	275	Morgan Tabb	373	John Ford
219	Samuel Jeanes	276	Morgan Tabb	403	Thomas Christie
220	Henry Saltus	277	James Watcher	404	Thomas Christie
221	James Read	278	James Watcher	431	Marmaduke Gerry
222	James Read	279	Francis Arthur	432	Marmaduke Gerry
223	Charles West	280	Francis Arthur	433	Marmaduke Gerry
224	Charles West	281	John Bryan	434	Robert Smallwood
225	John Shave	282	Samuel Richardson	435	Robert Smallwood
226	John Shave	283	John Gaspar Stirkey	436	John Winn
227	Richard Baker	284	John Gaspar Stirkey	437	Francis Arthur
228	Richard Baker	285	John Jones	438	Francis Arthur
229	Marn'k Perry	289	Thomas Carter	473	Francis Arthur
230	Marn'k Perry	290	Thomas Carter	474	Francis Arthur
231	Thomas Dunbar	305	Thomas Carter	475	Francis Arthur
232	Joshua Snowden	306	Thomas Carter	476	Francis Arthur
233	Samuel Burnley, Schmidt	307	Thomas Carter	477	Francis Arthur
234	Samuel Burnley, & Molich	308	Thomas Carter	478	Samuel Bacon
235	Samuel Burnley, Schmidt	309	Thomas Carter	479	Francis Lee
236	Samuel Burnley, & Molich	313	Samuel Tomlinson	480	John Tutes

GEORGIA'S ECONOMY

Great Britian's purpose in founding the American colonies was threefold;
  (1) Economic. Raw materials needed in England were to be grown in the colonies and shipped to Britian which in turn would export manufactured products to the colonies.
  (2) Strategic. Military bases were to be established and maintained to guard against foreign competitors.
  (3) Social. To provide a place where England's poor, unfortunate and rebellious citizens could be sent.

Since the function of a colony was to serve the mother-country, it naturally followed that the government and economy of that colony must be managed in accordance with the needs of England. While this concept was not necessarily bad, it did have one big fault. London, being 3,000 miles away, could not fully understand the conditions as they existed overseas, and had to make governmental decisions based on reports, propaganda and heresay. If a particular product was needed in England, it was easy to assume that product could be grown in the colonies, especially if no proof to the contrary existed.

Consequently a restrictive system was devised whereby economic bounties were offered for growing crops unsuited for certain soils. Four examples of this were found in Georgia where no amount of bounties could economically produce silk, wine, hemp or flax. The Georgia Assembly in 1767 not only offered bounties, but, free seed, to farmers to produce flax, but, to no avail.

On the whole, however, England's needs and Georgia's ability to produce meshed on most counts. Georgia had no difficulty growing rice, lumber, indigo, cotton and tobacco, and in securing deer skins for export from the Indians. Since Georgia had no manufacturing facilities, she purchased her manufactured products from England. She did produce a few crude items for plantation consumption like homespun cloth, stockings, shoes, some furniture and blacksmith products, but these were unimportant.

Georgia's economic field was three sided; agriculture, forest products, and Indian trade. Along the coast rice culture flourished. Indian corn and indigo grew on the high ground. In the upcountry wheat, Indian corn, tobacco, and a small amount of hemp was produced. Live stock prospered everywhere. The meat from cattle and hogs was salted, barrelled and exported. Lumber, produced along the coast was pine, oak, and cypress. Hardwoods and pine grew in the uplands. Lumber, turpentine, tar and pitch, shingles and barrel staves were produced and exported. Augusta was the center of the Indian trade, and in 1768, Georgia exported 300,000 pounds of deer skins, mostly to England.

However, it was the favorable trade balance with the West Indies that produced most of Georgia's hard money. There went rice, corn, peas, barrelled beef and pork, livestock, lumber, shingles and barrel staves. In return the West Indies sent rum, sugar, and a considerable amount of hard cash. England imported rice, indigo, lumber, naval stores and deer skins, and exported manufactured goods. The northern colonies imported little and exported fish and flour.

The trade balance with her northern neighbors was so unfavorable that Governor Wright publicly complained: "they take but little of our produce, and drain us of every trifle of gold and silver that is brought here, by giving a price for Guineas, Moidores, Johanne's Pistols and Dollars far above their real and intrinsic value, so we can never keep any amongst us."

In the value of imports and exports England was first, the West Indies second, and the northern colonies last. In 1773, a total of 216 trading vessels cleared through Georgia's only two ports at Savannah and Sunbury. Of this number 56 cleared Sunbury which accounted for roughly one-fourth of all trade.

According to Steven's History of Georgia, one-third of the wealth of the entire province was centered in St. John's parish. The commerce of this wealthy section passed through the port of Sunbury. Many of the ships that docked at Savannah moved partial cargoes back and forth in smaller boats to Sunbury. The town merchants dealt in all types of goods which at times might include slaves, clothing, books, hardware, flour, dried fish, medicine, Maderia wine, rum, kitchen ware, jewelry, guns and farm implements.

Newly arrived in Savannah from England, merchant Button Gwinnett placed the following ad in the Georgia Gazette, September 1765. "Just imported to be sold on the most reasonable terms by Button Gwinnett. Rhubarb, Dr. James' powders for fevers, mustard, tinware, plain silver and gold laced hats, silk and thread hose, jewelry, pickles, earthen and delftware, fine beer, Irish linens, cheese, butter, nails, bed-furniture . . . and many other articles too tedious to insert."

SUNBURY CHURCHES

At one time or another, Sunbury was served by three church denominations. These were Congregational, Episcopal and Baptist. At first, the Congregationalists living in Sunbury seem to have attended services at the Midway Church, but later had their own church and clergymen. The first record of this was an act by the legislature which chartered the Congregational Society of Sunbury in 1790. The Selectmen of the church were Frances Coddington, Davis Rees, James Powell and John Lawson. Services at Sunbury may have predated this act. Their organization was known as "Congregational Presbyterians," and was closely associated with the Midway Church. Ministers and members of the two churches were freely interchanged.

The Church of England, or Episcopal Church, was first served by a missionary, Reverend John Alexander, at Sunbury in 1766 and 1767. He was sent from London by the "Society for the Propagation of the Gospel in Foreign Parts." Reverend Alexander seems to have been disappointed and discouraged by this assignment. In two letters to Rev. Daniel Burton, D. D. of the Society, dated December 18, 1766 and February 7, 1767, he told of being taken sick five weeks after his arrival, August 2nd. He wrote that an epidemic was in full swing in Sunbury and that whole families were wiped out. His best friend and patron was among the dead.

He said land had been purchased in Florida and a new town was being laid out on the St. Johns River where the survivors of Sunbury were planning to move. He asked that the Society transfer him to Northwest North Carolina. He complained that he had not been furnished a church and had to conduct services in his own home.

He said the citizens were hostile "from the irreconcilable prejudices of Seducers and an insensed rable that join them in most abuses I have received from my first coming." He was transferred to Purisburg, South Carolina, late in 1767.

Another Society missionary at Savannah, Reverend Samuel Frink, seems to have had a very poor opinion of Rev. Alexander, calling him "that great deceiver," in a letter dated July 3, 1767.

After Rev. Alexander's departure, Sunbury was without a clergyman for several years. On July 8, 1771, a group of Episcopalian citizens sent the following petition for a new minister:

"Georgia
Parish of St. John's
Sunbury, 2 July 1771"

"To the Society for the Propagation of the Gospel in Foreign Parts. The Petition of part of the Inhabitants of said Parish in the Province aforesaid Humbly Slewth ....."

"That for some years past there has been no Clergyman to Perform devine service according to the rites and Ceremonies of the Church of England in Sunbury, a considerable Sea Port Town and a Port of Entry in said Province and Parish . . .

That a great part of the Inhabitants of said Parish are dissenters and that those who Profess the established Religion of the Church of England are not sufficient to maintain a Clergyman. That the sum allowed by the Province for the support of a Clergyman of the Church of England in said Parish is no more than Twenty five pounds Sterling yearly.

That His Excellency, James Wright Esqr. Governor of said Province, has been pleased at the request of Part of the Inhabitants of this Parish to appoint The Revd. Mr. Timothy Lowten to the Rector of the same and that this gentleman has Performed divine service according to the Rites and ceremonies of the Church of England in the Town of Sunbury for upwards of Three months past to the universal satisfaction of the Inhabitant and Parts adjacent.

That a number of Inhabitants have raised a further Sum for the support of Mr. Lowten for one year from the first of April Last but this is not sufficient and at best but Precarious and uncertain. We therefore, Your Petitioners, humbly beseech you will be pleased to appoint the said Mr. Lowten one of your Missionarys and allow him such a yearly salary as to you shall seem meet. & your Petitioners as in Duty bound shall Pray."

Signed:

"John Simpson
R. Kelsall
Thos. Young
Sutton Bankes
James Hardie
Fras. Coddington
Jeremiah Doulton
Samuel Morcock
John Cubbee
Wm. Anderson
John Lawson

Simon Munro
Samuel Miller
Andrew Darling
John Graves
Benj. Sheffield
Thomas Bilney
Thos. Maxwell
Wm. Clark
John Rose
Davis Austin
John Gibbons
Nath. Bacon

George Cubbed
Saml. Richardson
George Knowles
Peter Manley
Isaac Roberts
James Aitken
Nathan Saxton
Allan Stuart
Peter Bacon (deleted)
Jonathan Bacon
Donald Fraser
Thos. Bosomworth"

During most of 1771, Rev. Lowten was the missionary at Sunbury, and was well liked by the town as a whole. However, his stay was short. Late in 1771, Rev. Samuel Frink died in Savannah, and Rev. Lowten was transferred there to fill his position. There is no record of any other missionary being assigned to Sunbury.

The third religious denomination at Sunbury was the Baptist. In 1806, the Church was organized with the Reverend Charles Odingsell Screven as minister. The church building was imposing and was said to have been modelled after the church at Midway. According to Dr. Rufus W. Weaver, former President of Mercer University, it produced 25 Baptist ministers.

The Historic Preservation Section of the Georgia Department of Natural Resources believes the first Masonic meeting in Georgia was held at the future site of Sunbury, February, 1734. Oglethorpe and his men stopped there while exploring the coast searching for strategic fort locations. It is thought Oglethorpe served as Worshipful Master.

On April 21, 1777, St. John's Lodge Number Six of Sunbury, was chartered by the Grand Lodge of Georgia in Masonry 5777. On February 6, 1796, the Grand Lodge was incorporated and given power to corporate bodies under its jurisdiction by an act of the Georgia Legislature. With this new authority, Sunbury's Lodge Number Six was required to pay annual dues in arrearage to 1787. When this was done, the Lodge was admitted to full participation with the following officers recognized: Adam Alexander, Worshipful Master, William Peacock, Senior Warden, Andrew Maybank, Junior Warden, Thomas Lancaster, Treasurer, Daniel Stewart, Secretary, Nathan Dryer, Senior Deacon, John Bihlheimer, Junior Deacon, and James Robards and Samuel Law, Stewards. John and Rebecca Couper gave the Lodge lot number seventy-seven in Sunbury on which to build a lodge building, November 4, 1805.

The houses, stores and public building at Sunbury were built almost entirely of wood which was obtained easily from the nearby forest. Tabby, a natural mixture of cemented sea shells, was used for foundations, chimneys and out-buildings. The wharfs were made of palmetto pilings filled with shells, stones and tamped earth and sometimes covered with wooden flooring. Bricks were hard to get, although one firm in Savannah made

Typical Sunbury home was this raised-cottage made of timbers squared and fastened together and then covered with planks at the sides and ends. The roof was either shingled or boarded. The lower part of the house and chimneys were made of tabby, as were the out-houses and slave quarters. The porch areas were called piazzas or verandahs and were an important part of every home.

both brick and pottery. The bricks in the wall surrounding the Midway Cemetery were imported from England. The wall was completed in 1814 at a cost of $2,600 which was a lot of money in those days.

During colonial times life in Sunbury was slow and easy for the plantation owners and their families. Much time was spent in social affairs and in sailing, fishing, riding and hunting. There is no record of horse racing, although this sport was very popular in Savannah. There are no accurate records of Sunbury's population. C. C. Jones, Georgia historian, estimated it was about 1,000 in 1775.[1] It could have been more. When the outlying plantations added their population to the town, it must have been nearer 2,000.

Sunbury was one of the first Georgia towns to have a fashionable surburb. Many families desiring the convenience of a nearby town built their plantations on an off-shore strip of land about three miles wide which they named Bermuda Island after it's Caribbean counterpart. At one time six colonels owned homes here which eventually led to the changing of the islands name to Colonel's Island. This name it carries today.

Note: [1] The Dead Towns of Georgia, 1878

Following is an eye witness account of a visit paid to Sunbury in April, 1774 by botanist William Bartram, son of John Bartram of Philadelphia who had been appointed botanist to King George III in 1765. William Bartram, at the request of London, was to travel through North and South Carolina, Georgia and Florida "to explore the vegetable kingdom for the discovery of rare and useful productions of nature."[1]

On April 13, 1774, William Bartram recorded in his diary that he "Waited on his Excellency, the Governor (Governor James Wright of Georgia), who was pleased to receive me politely and offered to assist me all in his power."

On his visit to Midway and Sunbury William Bartram wrote:

"April 15th (1774). Bought a horse & the day following set out for the town of Sunbury. Rode 15 miles to Ferry on Great Ogeechee River. Crost the River & rode 15 miles to Midway Meeting house. Went into meeting being intraduced by some of my fellow Travilers being inhabitants of the part of the country. Heard a good sermon by Mr. Percey, a Methodist Missioner sent by the Count of Huntington (Rector of the Orphan Collige). This congregation was respectable & genteel. The Religious and Pious Sperit throughout the whole Audiance reflects a shining light on the Character of the inhabitants Midway & Newport.

After meeting rode nine miles to Sunbury. This Pretty Town is situated on the sound apposite St. Cathrine's Island & commands an agreeable prospect of the Inlet 4 or 5 miles from the Barr. There are about one hundred houses in the Town neatly built of wood framed having pleasant Piasas round them. The inhabitants are genteel & wealthy, either Merchants or Planters from the Country who resort here in the Summer & Autumn, to partake of the Salubrious Sea breeze, Bathing & sporting on the Sea Islands. The Barr is a good one. Vessel carrying 16 feet water over it. Here is a Custom house and Naval office for the incouragement of Commerce.

I went over to one of the Sea Islands, but discovered nothing new, or much worth your notice. On a high bluff observed a mound or Tumulous of Oister Shells; observed a clay urn, the shells being removed from it but found nothing in it but sand & dust. it was about 18 inches high & one foot in diameter, it was marked or carved on the outer surface in imitation of Basket work.

The vegitable Productions were the same as on other small Islands on the coast of Carolina and Georgia. The great Live Oak and dwarf evergreen Oaks, Water Oaks, Red Bay, Zanthoxilon, Frangula, Red Cedar, purple Berried Bay.

Note [1] Travels Through North and South Carolina and Georgia &c., 1792

Having received an invitation when in Savanna from one of the most considerable Planters in this part of the Province, I left the pleasant Town of Sunbury & went to his house. his Plantation is very large containing great quantities of Rice Land & being advantageously situated for the command of water over his Rice fields, he employs upwards of an hundred Negroes on this Plantation & expects to make 1600 Barrels of Rice this season.

His house is situated on a Peninsula of High Land which commands a most agreeable prospect of his vast extensive Rice fields which nearly sorounds him on all sides. he has no Orched of Fruit Trees which is a common neglect of the Planters through the Province.

Being invited by one of this gentleman's Neighbours I waited on him, who has likewise a large and well regulated Rice Plantation. stayed a few days in this settlement and was most hospitably entertained in the Family of the good Mr. B. Andrews, a member of the House of Assembly of this Province and a Worthy Elder of the Meeting in Midway Parish. During my stay here imployed my time in searching out the Natural productions of the country, took notice of a pretty species of Asphodelus called here by the inhabitants Floy poison, having a long loose spike of white Flowers. They gather the roots which they bruise & steep over night, in water, in which they put honey or Trekle, which they expose in a Broad dish or Platter on a Table in the Rooms of the house unto which the Flys swarm & almost instantly after taisting the fatal Nectar turn giddy & die in incredible numbers. on this account it is a most useful Plant in a Country so infested with these troublesome little Animals. The same too is used as effectively in destroying Crows, Rats & etc. Here, too, I observed the very singular species of Ledum or Adromeda, whose little white companulate Flowers, become monstrous excressances, every Part of the Flower inlarging proportionably & being of a deep flesh or rose colour afford a very agreeable appearance, some approching to the size of a Teacup and is on this account extremely singular & very beautiful. It is a very beautiful evergreen Shrub; the wood when dry being very solid close & fine grained & indures a polish resembling Box wood or Elder."

THE AMERICAN REVOLUTION

For the purpose of raising revenue in the American colonies, the British Parliament in 1765 passed the Stamp Act, which required the colonists to use stamped paper bought from the British government for legal documents, diplomas, and certificates. It further required that official Bristish stamps be affixed to newspapers, pamphlets, almanacs, calendars, playing cards and other articles. The purpose of the act was to raise money to pay for the French and Indian War, and to maintain military defenses in the provinces.

The act aroused immediate opposition among the colonists, who argued that Parliament could not legally tax them without their consent. To do so would be taxation without representation, and such duties would drain them of much of their specie and hard money in circulation in the colonies. Opposition was so violent that many British stamp agents were attacked by mobs and their property destroyed. The act proved to be of no monetary value to England since the collection of the tax amounted to more than the revenue produced. In 1766, the Stamp Act was repealed by Parliament, but, not until another measure called the Declaratory Act was passed, which affirmed Britian's right to legally pass acts binding on the colonists.

On May 13, 1769, Charles Townshend, leader of the British House of Commons, introduced three measures which became law:

(1) Suspension of the duties of the New York legislature.
(2) Establishment of a Commission of Customs to supervise laws relating to trade.
(3) Imposition of duties on tea, glass, paper, artist's materials, and red and white lead.

This act immediately revived the tax quarrel with Britian and proved to be another step on the road to war.

The Townshend Act caused little trouble in Georgia which imported but small amounts of these articles. However, in the other colonies, it caused great concern because it was again said to be taxation without representation. Like the Stamp Act before it, it proved to be a revenue dud and had an adverse effect on imports, since the colonists would not purchase these items. Parliament, in April 1770, repealed the act, but kept the tax on tea.

However, the Declaratory Act and the remaining tax on tea, which England tried to force the colonists to pay, resulted in the Boston Tea Party, in December 1773. A shipload of tea was dumped into the harbour by the aroused Bostonians who refused to let it land and be taxed.

To punish this defiance, Parliament, in the spring of 1774, passed four really repressive acts which came to be known as the "Intolerable Acts" by all Americans.
   (1) The port of Boston was to be closed until the East India Company was paid for the dumped tea.
   (2) Certain powers were taken away from the Massachusetts Assembly and given to the Governor.
   (3) Officials could be tried in London for accusations made in the colonies against them.
   (4) The expense of quartering British troops in Boston was to be borne by that colony.

Such obvious acts of coercion, plus the presence of British troops in Boston, were a red flag waved to all Americans. Virginia immediately sent invitations to the other colonies to attend an inter-colonial Congress to appraise the situation. South Carolina reacted with a call for a general meeting to be held in Charleston, July 6-8, 1774, to make its resolutions concerning the Intolerable Acts and to select delegates to the Congress.

In the July 14th issue of the Georgia Gazette, published in Savannah, an invitation appeared inviting delegates from all Georgia parishes to assemble at Tondee's Tavern in Savannah, July 27, 1774 to consider the serious threat to America caused by the passage of the acts. The printed invitation was signed by George Walton, Noble W. Jones, Archibald Bulloch, and John Houstoun.

Georgia's reaction was by no means one-sided disapproval of England. Many citizens thought the Creek Indians were a greater menace to her frontiers than the British, whose troops in St. Augustine were a comforting assurance against attack. Others said the Bostonians should pay for the tea and forget it.

On July 27, when the delegates arrived at Savannah for the meeting, it was discovered that some of the more distant parishes were not represented. These had been too far away to allow for selection of delegates, and for making the long trip to Savannah. The meeting was adjourned and a new assembly date set for August 10. Of the delegates that did attend, thirty were selected as a committee to draw up resolutions condemning the Intolerable Acts to be presented to the meeting on August 10.

Just how many people attended the July 27 meeting was not recorded, but a Charleston newspaper estimated that about one hundred came from one parish, believed to have been St. John's, bearing a resolution not to buy or use British goods until the rights of Americans were restored.

St. John's Parish because of its independence of thought and the religious beliefs of its New England Congregationalists had never been on the inside with the British "court party" in Savannah, but remained aloof retaining what Governor Wright called "Oliverian principles." This reference was to Oliver Cromwell, Protector of England, 1599-1658, who espoused the Puritan cause and mounted protests against abuses of the church and state under King Charles I.

At the August 10 meeting, every parish was represented in spite of a proclamation issued by Governor Wright warning that such a meeting was unconstitutional and punishable by law. Resolutions adopted at the meeting covered the following ground:

(1) Americans were entitled to all the rights and privileges and immunities of British citizens.
(2) Americans had indisputable right to petition the British throne.
(3) The Boston Port Bill was contrary to the British constitution because it deprived people of their property without a jury trial, punished both the innocent and the guilty, and was "ex post facto" law.
(4) The absolution of the Massachusetts charter subverted American rights.
(5) Parliament lacked the power to tax the colonies since the British constitution did not permit taxation without representation.
(6) The only proper method to raise tax funds was through the colonial assemblies.
(7) It was unjust and unlawful to transport a suspected person to England for trial, away from the locality where the crime was said to have occured. This deprived the suspected person of local witnesses and a trial by his peers.

The Georgia appeal based its trust on the constitutional rights of the colonies against the unconstitutional acts of Parliament. The meeting debated sending delegates to a Congress of all colonies to be held in Philadelphia, but finally decided against it. The reason is not clear. A second attempt to get approval to send delegates was made by the St. John's Parish members before adjournment, but this failed to get a majority vote, also. Consequently when the First Continential Congress met in Philadelphia, September 5, 1774, only 12 colonies were represented.

When St. John's Parish failed to get approval to send delegates from the whole province, its citizens resolved to send representatives anyway. Two meetings were called at Midway, attended by delegates from St. John's, St. Andrew's, St. George's and St. David's parishes. At the second meeting, Dr. Lyman Hall from Sunbury was elected to attend the First Continental Congress, but he did not go to Philadelphia, probably because he felt he did not have sufficient backing to be accepted there.

When the Continental Congress met, without Georgia, it agreed to boycott British imports and to forego exports. It recommended the use of force to resist efforts by England to impose its taxation measures. Although Georgia was not a party to these resolutions, St. John's Parish immediately began a movement to adopt the boycott and to espouse the other objectives of the Contintental Association.

On December 3, 1774, a committee appointed at the August 10 meeting in Savannah sent invitations to all parishes to elect delegates to attend a Provincial Congress to meet in Savannah at the same time the Georgia Assembly was to meet there. The Assembly met, January 17, 1775 and the Provincial Congress the next day.

Five parishes sent delegates to the Congress, St. Paul's, St. Andrew's, St. Mathew's, St. George's and Christ Church. St. John's Parish refused to attend until the Provincial Congress agreed to join the Continental Association. This they agreed to do, with modifications. It was to become effective on March 15, 1775. The non-consumption agreement was ignored, Georgia was to continue trade with the other colonies such as the West Indies, even though they were trading with England. Merchandise needed for Georgia's Indian trade was to continue to be imported from England pending a decision by the next Continental Congress.

It was agreed, with the exemptions mentioned, not to import any goods from England, Ireland, British West Indies or to accept African slaves after March 1, 1775. All exports to these places were to stop, December 1, 1775. Local manufacturing was to be encouraged. The merchants agreed not to raise prices which seems to have been the first time voluntary price controls were considered in America. Amusements and all unnecessary expenditures were to stop.

A paid committee was to be elected in every town, district, and parish to see that the Association agreements were adhered to. American ship captains were forbidden to take on boycotted goods. The custom house records for the ports of Sunbury and Savannah were to be inspected, and violators were to be publicly exposed. A record of their offenses were to be sent to the other colonies.

Before adjourning, the Provinical Congress elected John Houstoun, Archibald Bulloch and Noble W. Jones to attend the Second Continental Congress to be held in Philadelphia in May 1775. They never went. When the Congress adjourned it left final approval of its actions up to the General Assembly which couldn't agree. On February 10, 1775, the last Georgia Assembly to meet adjourned bitterly divided.

The citizens of St. John's Parish were so put out at this display of pussyfooting that they elected Dr. Lyman Hall, Sunbury's leading physician, to attend the Continental Congress in Philadelphia, independently of the rest of Georgia. Hall was born in Wallingford, Connecticut in 1724. In 1747 he graduated from Yale and became an ordained minister of the Fairfield West Consociation in Bridgeport. He gave up preaching for medicine and in his early thirties moved to Dorchester, South Carolina. When these New England Congregationalists moved their colony to Midway, Georgia, he came along. At Sunbury, Hall was probably the hottest advocate of the revolutionary cause. When he arrived at the Continental Congress in Philadelphia, he was unanimously accepted, but he refused to vote because each colony had but one vote, and he represented only a single Georgia parish.

In early 1775, Governor Wright and the Crown were having real trouble enforcing their authority. When the tax collector at Savannah seized eight hogsheads of molasses and six others of French sugar, for non-payment of taxes, a mob disguised as sailors in blackface raided the wharf and carted the merchandise away. Of the three guards on duty, one was tarred and feathered and the other two were thrown into the river. One supposedly drowned.

At Sunbury on June 26, the schooner "Lively" arrived with illegal goods aboard. James Kitching, the tax collector, seized the vessel and sent the comptroller and searcher, Mr. Antrobus, aboard to decommission it. A group of Sunbury citizens gathered and ordered Mr. Antrobus to leave town. He refused and was forcibly removed. The ropes were then cast off and the crew sailed out into St. Cathrine's Sound.[1] The record did not

Note: [1] The Dead Towns of Georgia, 1878

give its distination, but it probably unloaded its cargo elsewhere along the Georgia coast.

Collector Kitching applied to the local magistrate to take some action against the Sunbury citizens who had taken part in the episode. He did nothing. The deputy provost marshal was threatened when he attempted to serve writs against the offenders. He could do nothing.

As the spirit of revolution quickened, Governor Wright repeatedly called on London to send military reinforcements to Georgia. Early in 1775, 100 British troops and a small cruiser were ordered to Savannah from St. Augustine. The Governor, after meeting with his council, decided 100 troops were not enough, and their presence, he felt, would cause more resentment among the Whigs then they could control. Consequently, the Governor stopped their transfer and urgently requested London to furnish 500 troops. Before his request could be acted upon, news of the battles at Lexington and Concord reached Savannah on May 10.

By July, the revolutionary viewpoint was so pronounced, Governor Wright requested that he be returned to England. He stated in his request he could no longer stand the insults being hurled at him, and that he was powerless to control the rebellious activities of the people.

When the Declaration of Independence was signed, July 4, 1776, three Georgians affixed their signatures. Two of the signers, Lyman Hall and Button Guinnett were from Sunbury, and the third signer, George Walton, was later held prisioner there after his capture at Savannah when that city fell into British hands in 1779.

GEORGIA PREPARES FOR WAR

When it became evident that war with England was coming, the citizens of Sunbury and St. John's parish began military training. Some joined the Georgia militia, some the regular Colonial forces, and still others formed an infantry company and a troop of cavalry for local defenses. Four officers who thus participated and later distinguished themselves in the war were Colonels Andrew and Cooper Maybank, Colonel John Baker and Major Charles West.

For the protection of Sunbury, a fort was built 500 yards south of the town, on a bluff which sloped down to the salt marshes separating it from Colonel's Island. In front of the fort

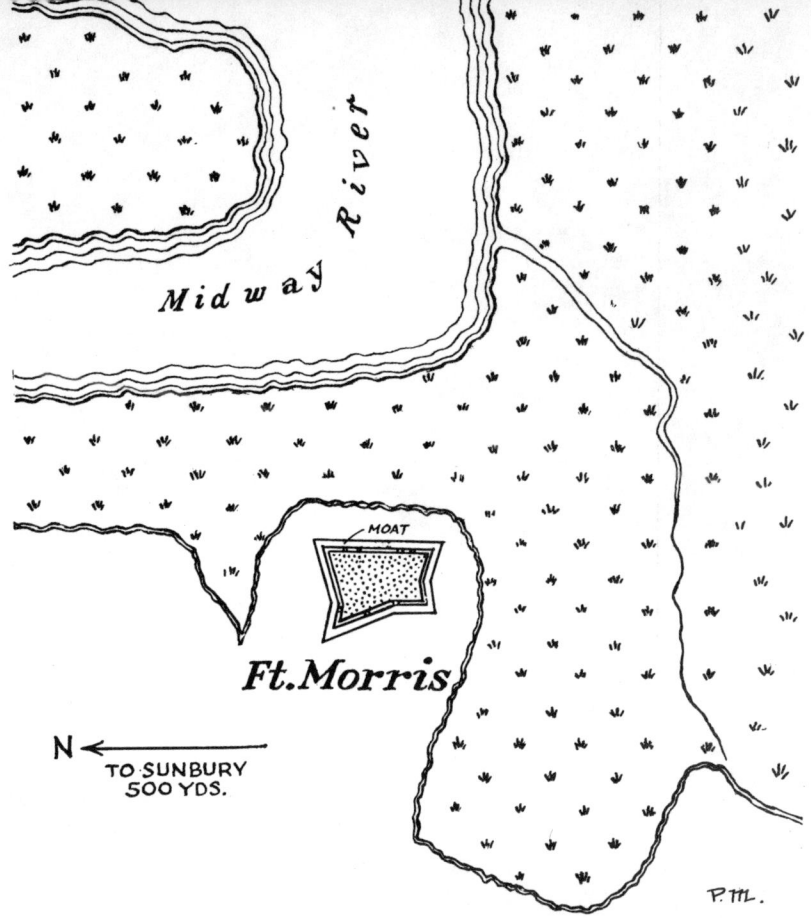

were more marshes extending to the mouth of the Midway River which turned north out of St. Cathrine's Sound and flowed past Sunbury. The fort was designed not only to protect against an attack from the sea, but against an attack mounted from the north by ships that might have slipped up the river. It was also designed to combat an attack by land from the rear.

Any landing of infantry from in front of the fort was nearly impossible since such troops would have had to struggle through waist deep marshes. The same can be said for a an attack from the south. Only from the north and west would an assault by ground forces be prudent.

The construction of Fort Morris was a very substantial earthwork which surrounded a parade of about an acre. Facing the river, eastward, it measured 275 feet in length. Here the biggest guns, or 24 pounders, were located. On the northern side, it measured 191 feet, on the west 240 feet, and on the southern side only 140 feet, which made it an irregular

Mouth of the Midway River as seen from Fort Morris.

rectangle. The short southern side was probably due to the fact that no attack was expected from the marshes there.

It was defended by 25 pieces of ordnance made up of 4, 6, 9, 12, 18 and 24 pounders. The smaller caliber guns predominated. It was believed some of these guns had been taken from Fort Frederica on St. Simon's Island near Brunswick. The Georgia Safety Council had ordered this badly neglected fort secured. These guns were mounted "en barbette" meaning they were mounted on platforms so they could be fired over the walls of the fort.

C. C. Jones, Georgia historian, visited the abandoned and decayed fort about 1877 and wrote: "Seven embrasures may still be seen, each about five feet wide. The parapet, ten feet wide, rises six feet above the parade of the fort, and its superior slope is about twenty-five feet above the level of the river at high tide. Surrounding the work is a moat, at present ten feet deep, ten feet wide at the bottom, and twice that width at the top. Near the middle of the curtain may be seen traces of a sally-port or gateway fifteen feet wide."

"Such is the appearance of this abandoned work as ascertained by a recent survey. Completely overgrown by cedars, myrtles and vines, its presence would not be suspected, even at a short remove, by those unacquainted with the locality. Two iron cannons are now lying half buried in the loose soil of the parade, and a third will be found in the old field about midway between the fort and the town."[1]

Note: [1] The Dead Towns of Georgia, 1878

32

A view of the moat surrounding Fort Morris before restoration was begun

When I visited the fort site in 1969, I found it much as C. C. Jones had described it nearly a hundred years earlier with the exception that the three guns he spoke of were buried or gone. In 1940 one gun was excavated and is now mounted on the Court House lawn at Hinesville, Ga. Inside the parade, I found a few old bricks which were probably a part of an amunition storehouse or a cooking oven. Blowing sand has obliterated many details of construction and hidden artifacts.

Some kind of earlier fort may have been built on the same site. According to the Record Book of the Midway Church, a warning letter was received by the congregation in 1756, from the honorable Jonathan Bryan, a member of the governor's council for the Province saying the Indians were greatly disturbed over the killing of several of their tribe by settlers on the Ogeechee River in a dispute over cattle. He advised the Midway community to build a fort for protection. In response to the warning, a site was chosen on land owned by Captain Mark Carr at the future site of Sunbury. Why this location was chosen is a mystery since it was eleven miles from Midway. In case of a sudden Indian attack most of the inhabitants could not have reached it in time. Work on this fort was begun, September 20, 1756. No other information could be found. If it was built on the future site of Fort Morris, verification will have to await excavation.

33

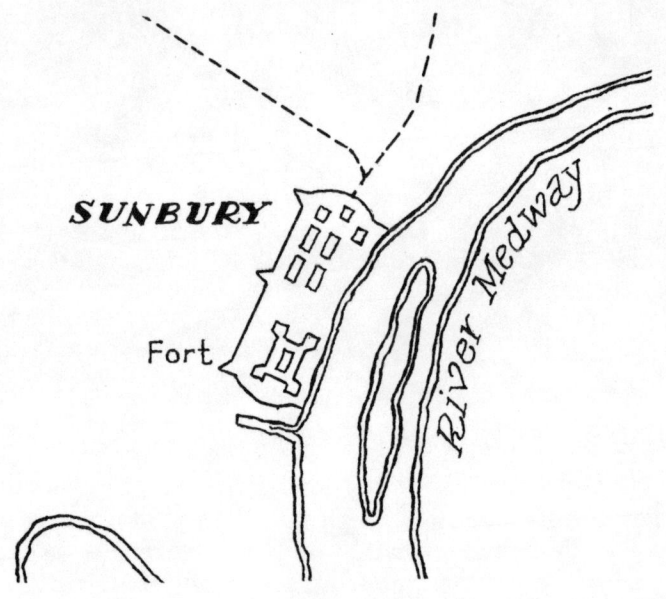

There are many unanswered questions about the Fort Morris of the American Revolution. When was construction begun and when was the fort completed? What was the configuration and size of the fort? The map above was redrawn by the author from a section of a map published in London in 1780. This map, "SKETCH OF THE NORTHERN FRONTIERS OF GEORGIA," by Lt. Col. Archibald Campbell, shows both Sunbury and Fort Morris protected by what appears to be a palisade. Was this constructed of tree trunks sharpened on top to impede entry or escape?

It is known that Sunbury was used by the British, after its capture in 1779, as a prisoner of war camp. Did the British construct the wall with prison labor to thwart escape, or was it constructed prior to that time by the Americans for protection against British attack?

The Campbell map shows Fort Morris with what appears to be turrets positioned at all four corners. The purpose of this configuration was to make possible firing in two directions at once. This was the usual type of Revolutionary War construction. The map on page 31, shows a fort of a different shape. It is known that Fort Morris was rebuilt during the War of 1812. At this time was its configuration changed to a modified star shape because of its marshy location which made it practically invulnerable to ground attack except from the rear?

The Continental Congress in session in Philadelphia, on the day following the signing of the Declaration of Independence, resolved to raise two battalions to serve in Georgia. Blank military commissions were sent to Georgia to be filled in with the names of qualified leaders. The Legislatures of Virginia and the Carolinas were asked to allow enlistments for these two Georgia battlions from their citizens. Four galleys were to be built for defense of the Georgia coast, and two artillery companies were to be recruited and stationed in the forts at Sunbury and Savannah.

The exact date when construction began on Fort Morris is not known. The labor to build the fort was supplied by the slaves from nearby plantations. Captain Morris was the first commander, but the day his command began is not known. It had to be prior to December 5, 1777 when the following order from Colonel Samuel Elbert, Continental Commander in Savannah, was issued:

"Orders to Captain Defatt of the Artillery"

"You are to proceed immediately to the Town of Sunbury, in this State, where are a corps of Continental Artillery posted, which you are constantly to be employed in teaching the perfect use of Artillery, particularily in the Field. Both Officers and Men are hereby strictly ordered to attend on you for the purpose, at such times and in such places as you may direct; and the Commanding Officer of the Troops in that place on your showing him these Orders, will furnish Men to so the necessary duty in the Town & Fort; so that there will be nothing to prevent Captain Morris and his Company from being perfect in the business for which they were raised. Such pieces of Artillery as you approve of, have mounted on Field-Carrages; and for this purpose you are empowered to employ the necessary Workmen, and procure Materials. Your drafts on me for every necessary Expense, accompanying the Vouchers, will be duly honored."

"I am, Sir, your most Obdt. Servt.,
S. Elbert, Col Command'g."

The Continental Congress, on February 27, 1776, created a Southern Military Department which included Georgia, North Carolina, and Virginia. Major General Charles Lee was named Commander. South Carolina was under the separate command of Brigadier General John Armstrong.

In 1776, South Georgia was being harrassed by raiding parties of horsemen called the Florida Rangers. The purpose of their raids was to steal cattle and food and to plunder the unprotected plantations for the benefit of the considerable number of Loyalists in North Florida who had fled from Georgia and South Carolina. The leader of the Florida Rangers was Thomas Brown who had been tarred and feathered in Augusta as a British sympathizer.

It was estimated that Georgia had only 4,000 able-bodied men in its militia, and if all these were to be used in defense of its borders, the Georgia economy would collapse for lack of manpower. 2,000 was considered the top number it could call for duty at any one time.

To meet the threat of the Florida Rangers and the British regular troops at St. Augustine, General Lee mapped plans for an attack on Florida. Since Georgia lacked the manpower for such a drive, additional troops from Virginia and North Carolina were ordered to rendezvous at Sunbury. Records show that these troops, immediately on arrival, were stricken with what was called "fevers". So serious was this outbreak of sickness that 10 to 15 troops were dying daily. To save the army, the troops were transported to the offshore islands away from Sunbury. All through the history of Sunbury and Midway was found accounts of fevers, pleurisies and epidemics killing great numbers of people. This terrific amount of sickness certainly was one contributing factor in the eventual death of the town.

After much difficulty in collecting men, supplies, and transportation, General Lee's expedition to Florida began uncertainly in September. So poorly organized was the venture that few troops got any further south than the St. John's River. Governor Tonyn of Florida said the troops never left Sunbury. The venture was a military fiasco. Reasons given for the failure were sick troops, insufficient transportation, lack of cooperation between the military and civilian leaders, hostility of the Indians, and lack of motivation of the Americans when they learned St. Augustine had been recently reinforced.

General Lee was reassigned, and was succeeded by General Robert Howe as Continental Commander in the South. On arrival in Savannah in March 1777, General Howe conferred with Governor Button Gwinnett, who had just been commissioned President of the State of Georgia and Commander-in-Chief of the Army upon the sudden death of Governor Archibald Bullock.

Gwinnett felt a Florida invasion was necessary and would be successful if properly supplied. General Howe felt he lacked the necessary logistics, and that the time of year was wrong for an invasion. Gwinnett was dictatorial and hard to get along with. He believed General Howe was contemptous of his civilian background, even though he was Commander-in-Chief of the Georgia forces. At any rate, General Howe refused to commit South Carolina troops for a Florida invasion, although he did send a battalion to Sunbury. The rest of the troops General Lee had assembled he ordered back to Charleston.

Governor Gwinnett was disappointed, but he was not discouraged and went ahead with plans for the Florida invasion. The First Georgia Battalion of 400 men were at his disposal, and he called up the Georgia militia of about 2,000 men. Only about 200 of these actually reported for duty. The Georgia Navy which consisted of seven armed galleys was alerted. The First Georgia Battalion was under Continental control and commanded by General Lachlan McIntosh, a very able military man, but as headstrong as Gwinnett. Bitter rivalry broke out as to who should be in command of the expedition.

Early, Governor Tonyn of Florida learned of the plans for this new attack against St. Augustine through British sympathizers. He called on the Creek and Cherokee Indians to attack the Georgia frontiers and redoubled his efforts to get the displaced Loyalists from Georgia and South Carolina to join the British regulars in defense of St. Augustine.

Early in April 1777, the Georgia militia and the Continental troops moved to Sunbury in preparation for the invasion. Here Gwinnett and McIntosh locked horns again, each insisting he was the legal leader of the expedition. Since neither would give in, the Georgia Safety Council advised both to step aside, which they did. Colonel Samuel Elbert, the ranking Continental officer, then took command.

The expedition moved out May 1. Colonel Elbert and his Continental troops sailed down the inland waterway. Colonel John Baker and a group of mounted militia went by land. After entering Florida, the militia crossed the Nassau River and at Thomas Creek were met by the British Regulars, Florida Rangers and Indian supporters. Here they were defeated, May 17, 1777. This was the southernmost battle of the Revolution. The battlefield is located about 25 miles north of Jacksonville, on the west side of Interstate 95, south of the Nassau River. Colonel Elbert's flotilla, on reaching the Amelia Narrows, just below the St. Mary's River, found its vessels could not pass. With many of his troops sick and discouraged, and with food running low, Colonel Elbert turned back. On June 15, he was back in Savannah, after leaving off Colonel McIntosh at Sunbury with 127 men to defend the town and fort.

The bitterness that existed between Governor Gwinnett and General McIntosh was fanned still further when a brother, George McIntosh, a member of the Georgia Safety Council, was arrested on orders from Gwinnett and put in irons in a common jail. The arrest resulted from a recommendation from the Continental Congress following interception of a letter from Florida's Governor Tonyn. The letter said that George McIntosh was a British sympathizer. There was much conflicting evidence, but it seemed George McIntosh helped load a vessel with rice at Darien, supposedly headed for Dutch Guiana in May 1776. William Panton, a known Loyalist, was aboard the ship which went to St. Augustine. There it got new papers and proceeded to the West Indies where the rice was sold and a cargo picked up for St. Augustine. No one could actually prove George McIntosh was guilty of anything other than stupidity, but for a member of the Safety Council to act so foolishly was almost unpardonable.

Gwinnett considered the charges treasonable and refused George McIntosh bail. This decision was reversed by the Governor's Council in Gwinnett's absense and McIntosh was released on bail. Some said three of McIntosh's relatives were on the Council. George McIntosh was taken under guard to Philadelphia for a hearing before the Continental Congress, October 2-10, 1777. The decision was that not enough evidence was presented to hold him for trial, so he was released.

When the Georgia Assembly met in early 1777, it took up the Florida exposition fiasco and attempted to decide which was more culpable, Gwinnett or Lochlan McIntosh. It decided in favor of Gwinnett. This decision so enraged General McIntosh that he arose in the Assembly and called Gwinnett "A scoundrel and a lying rascal."[1] Gwinnett challenged McIntosh to a duel, which was held on the outskirts of Savannah, May 16. Both men were wounded, but Gwinnett died three days later.

No record can be found as to where he was buried. Some historians have guessed Savannah. There is just a good reason to believe he lies in the abandoned cemetery at Sunbury. Certainly some of his happiest days were spent here before the war when he was a plantation owner on St. Cathrine's Island and a

Note: [1] G. F. Jenkins, Button Gwinnett, 1926

Is Button Gwinnett buried here in the old abandoned Sunbury Cemetery?

Sunbury Justice of the Peace. Sunbury being but 28 miles from Savannah, his body could have been sent there for burial in a day or two down the coastal waterway.

Button Gwinnett was born, May 16, 1735 at Down Hatherly, Gloucestershire, England. His father was a clergyman. His mother was from a family of consequence in Herefordshire. For several years, he was engaged in exporting goods to the American colonies. In 1765 he came to America and settled in Savannah. A short time later, in October, 1765, he purchased St. Cathrine's Island off the coast from Sunbury and became a plantation owner. In 1767 and 1768, he was a Justice of the Peace in Sunbury. In January 1776, he attended a meeting of the Georgia Safety Council and was elected a delegate to the Continental Congress in Philadelphia. He was one of the three Georgia signers of the Declaration of Independence. On the sudden death of Governor Archibald Bulloch, he was commissioned, "President of the State of Georgia." Two months later he was defeated when he ran for Governor. His ambition was to be a military general, and this led to his quarrel with General McIntosh which resulted in his death by duel. His relatives are extinct, and no reliable portrait of Gwinnett exists. Is he buried at Sunbury? A metal sign erected by the State of Georgia outside the abandoned cemetery says that markers of colonial dead were removed prior to 1870. Perhaps some day careful excavation of the site will furnish the answer.

At the next meeting of the Assembly, General McIntosh was arrested, tried and acquitted for his part in Gwinnett's death. However, resentment was so great throughout Georgia that his usefulness as Commander of the Georgia Continental brigade was in doubt. George Walton and his friends in the Continental Congress came to his aid and he was reassigned. On August 6, 1777, he was ordered to report to General George Washington. At Valley Forge during the awful winter of 1777 and 1778 he was in charge of a 150 man detail entrusted with the personal safety of Washington whose life was in constant danger from his freezing troops. He served with distinction.

Early in 1778 a third expedition against St. Augustine was planned and attended by the usual civilian-military quarreling over leadership. General Howe thought it unwise to attack at that time. Governor Houstoun, believing an attack on Georgia from St. Augustine was in the making, thought it should be made immediately.

By the first of May, 2,000 troops had been gathered. The Continentals under the leadership of General Howe, the Georgia militia under the command of Governor Houstoun, the South Carolina militia under Colonel Andrew Williamson, and the naval units under Commander Oliver Bowen. General Howe believed he should lead, being the top ranking officer in the Continental Southern command. Governor Houstoun, barely 30 years old and with no military training, would not take orders from Colonel Howe. Commander Bowen would take orders from no one since it could not be decided if his vessels were under Continental or Georgia State control.

The leadership squabble continued, even though the expedition began moving. It reached the St. Mary's River, June 29. The Florida Rangers destroyed their own supplies, fell back on Fort Tonyn, destroyed that and retreated further into Florida. At this point General Howe, with the approval of the Continental officers, decided to abandon the expedition, and returned to Savannah, July 15. Governor Houstoun and Colonel Williamson decided they had insufficient troops left to continue their advance, so they returned to Savannah also. Thus ended the third attempt to invade Florida and like the two previous tries, it was a military fiasco.

BRITISH OCCUPATION OF GEORGIA

The British plan for a Southern campaign was mapped by Lord George Germain in 1778 and called for an early capture of Savannah. As a diversion to the main attack coming by sea from New York, a drive called for the capture of Sunbury and Fort Morris. General Augustine Prevost, Commander at St. Augustine, sent a two pronged drive north. His brother, Lieutenant Colonel Mark Prevost with 100 British Regulars and 300 Loyalists and Indians marched overland. Lieutenant Colonel Fuser, with a detachment of infantry and light artillery was dispatched by sea. On November 19, Colonel Prevost entered South Georgia and began looting and destroying the plantations. All able bodied men were taken prisoners.

Colonel John Baker hastily collected a band of mounted militia and advanced along the Savannah-Darien road to meet Colonel Prevost and his men. At Bulltown swamp a skirmish took place and the Americans retreated. Colonel Baker, Captain Cooper and William Goulding were wounded. Further along the way, at the Riceboro Bridge, another brief engagement occurred, but this encounter was too feeble to materially slow Prevost's advance.

At the Midway Meeting House, Colonel John White, Commander of the Continental troops stationed at Sunbury arrived with about 100 men and two pieces of artillery. He hastily constructed a crude breastwork across the road hoping to halt Prevost long enough for reinforcements to arrive from Savannah. A messenger had been dispatched to advise Colonel Elbert of the invasion. Major William Baker, with a party of horse militia, was sent ahead to harrass the enemy and slow his advance wherever possible.

On the morning of the 24th, General Screven with twenty militia troops joined Colonel White. After consultation, it was decided the best defensive position was a mile and a half below the Midway Meeting House where the road passed through a thickly wooded area and where an ambush could be laid.

With Colonel Prevost was a Loyalist from Georgia who was also familiar with the Midway section, and he too suggested that the British set up an ambush at the same spot. The two forces met and fighting began. General Screven was wounded, fell into enemy hands and died. Colonel Prevost's horse was shot from under him, and both horse and rider fell. Major Roman, in charge of the two artillery pieces brought from Sunbury, thought Prevost dead and moved his guns forward. Major James Jackson, believing victory certain, gave a lusty victory yell.

This was the same James Jackson, later promoted to Lieutenant Colonel, who was selected by General Anthony Wayne, in July 1783, to lead the occupying American forces back into Savannah after the British withdrawal. Later he was elected Governor of Georgia by the Assembly, but refused to serve saying he was too young and inexperienced for such a high office. This display of modesty has never since been equalled in American politics. Later James Jackson was elected United States Senator, accepted, and served until his death.

Major Jackson's victory yell proved premature, as Colonel Prevost reappeared on a fresh horse and continued his advance. Breaking down the bridge across the swamp, Colonel White retreated past the Midway Meeting House several miles down the Savannah road. Here he prepared a false letter supposedly written to him by Colonel Elbert from Savannah saying a large body of American cavalry had crossed the Ogeechee River and would circle around to Colonel Prevost's rear. The false letter advised Colonel White to continue his retreat and draw Prevost further into the trap.

It is believed this letter, which was dropped at a conspicuous place in the road, was found and delivered to Colonel Prevost who thought it genuine. At any rate, he halted his advance about six miles north of the Midway Meeting House. Meanwhile, a scouting party sent to Sunbury to ascertain if Colonel Fuser and his expedition had arrived by sea, returned with the information they were nowhere to be found. This information, along with a scout report that Colonel Elbert had reinforced Colonel White at the Ogeechee ferry, so discouraged Colonel Prevost that he returned to St. Augustine.

On the way, he burned the Midway Meeting House, all homes and negro dwellings, rice barns and plundered the plantation of every valuable that could be transported. The desolation caused by Colonel Prevost was described in a poem written by the son of Colonel John Baker.[1]

> "Where'er they march, the buildings burn
> Large stacks of rice to ashes turn
> And me (Midway) a pile of ruin made
> Before their hellish malice staid

Note: [1] The Dead Towns of Georgia, 1878

> Nor did their boundless fury spare
> The house devote to God and prayer
> Brick, coal, and ashes shew the place
> Which once the sacred house did grace
>
> The churchyard, too, no better sped
> The rabble so against the dead
> Transported where with direful fumes
> They tore up and uncovered tombs."

The flotilla bearing Colonel Fuser, 500 men, mortars, light artillery and battering cannon arrived off Sunbury late in November, having been delayed by storms. It anchored at the shipyard on Colonel's Island, seven miles south of Fort Morris. Here they disembarked, and the foot soldiers with their ordnance began to march to Sunbury. The armed vessels then sailed up the Midway River and took up positions opposite Sunbury and the fort. Colonel Fuser sent the following ultimatum to Colonel John McIntosh who held Fort Morris with 127 Continental troops and an undetermined number of militia and Sunbury volunteers.

"Sir,"

"You cannot be ignorant that four armies are in motion to reduce this Province. One is Already under the guns of your fort, and may be joined, when I think proper, by Colonel Prevost who is now at the Medway meetinghouse. The resistance you can, or intend to make, will only bring destruction upon this country. On the contrary, if you will deliver me the fort which you command, and lay down your arms and remain neuter until the fate of America is determined, You shall, as well as all the inhabitants of this parish, remain in peaceable possession of your property. Your answer, which I expect in an hour's time, will determine the fate of this country, whether it is to be laid in ashes, or remain as above proposed."

"I am Sir,
   Your most obedient, &c.,
                           L. V. Fuser
                     Colonel 60th Regiment and Commander
                     of his Majesty's Troops in Georgia,
                     on his Majesty's Service."

"P.S.

Since this letter was closed, some of your people have been firing scattering shot about the line. I am to inform you, that if a stop is not put to such irregular proceeding, I shall burn a house for every shot fired."

To this ultimatum, Colonel McIntosh replied:

"Sir,

We acknowledge we are not ignorant that your army is in motion to endeavour to reduce this State. We believe it entirely chimerical that Colonel Prevost is at the Meeting-House: but should it be so, we are in no degree apprehensive of danger from a junction of his army and yours. We have no property compared with the object we contend for that we value as such a rush: —and would rather perish in a vigorous defence than accept of your proposals. We sir, are fighting the battles of America, and therefore disdain to remain neuter till its fate is determined. As to surrendering the fort, receive this laconic reply: "COME AND TAKE IT." Major Lane, whom I send with this letter, is directed to satisfy you with respect to the irregular, loose firing mentioned on the back of your letter.

I have the honor to be Sir,
Your most obedient Servant,

John McIntosh,
Colonel of Continental Troops."

When Major Lane met Colonel Fuser he said the small arms fire that the Colonel had complained about was being maintained to keep Fuser's troops from entering and plundering Sunbury. He said that Colonel McIntosh was not frightened by his threat to burn the town and if he was so uncivilized, he would apply the torch at his end of town whenever Colonel Fuser fired his end and let the flames meet.[1]

Colonel Fuser did not begin the attack right away, but he waited for his scouts to return from Midway with the news of Colonel Prevost's whereabouts. When they returned with the information that Colonel Prevost had given up the attack and returned to St. Augustine, he was dismayed. Not willing to apply but one half of the pinchers movement, with Prevost's half missing, he withdrew the siege and returned to Florida.

Bitter recriminations followed with Colonel Prevost blaming Colonel Fuser for his late arrival, and Fuser blaming Prevost for running away. Considering the size of either force, Fort Morris would certainly have fallen had either attacked.

Note: [1] White's Historical Colletions of Georgia, 1855
McCall's History of Georgia, Vol.II, 1816

Shortly, thereafter, General Howe, having collected his forces, marched to Sunbury after the siege had been lifted. He proceeded to find fault with everything there instead of trying to improve an admittedly bad defensive posture. He seemed to have been a disciplinarian, however, having issued the following General Order, January 16, 1778, extracted:

"Complaints have been made to the General that some of the Soldiers have injured the Buildings in the Town; and his own observation convinces him that these complaints are but too well founded. Action like these disgrace an army, and render it hateful. Any soldier who either offers Insult or does Injury to the Persons or Property of the Inhabitants will be punished in the severest manner. And officers of every degree are injoined to exert themselves to prevent such enormities for the future if possible, or to detect those who commit them, that they may receive that punishment which such Actions so richly deserve. Officers of Companies are to take particular care that their men are made acquainted with this Order."

The main part of the British drive against Georgia was under the command of Colonel Campbell and was composed of about 3,000 men. It was made up of two regiments of Hessians, two battalions of the 71st Scottish Regiment, three or four battalions of New York Loyalists, and one detachment of artillery.

On November 27, 1778, it sailed from New York, but ran into a storm and was forced to return to Staten Island for repairs. It set sail again and arrived at Tybee Island off the coast from Savannah on Debember 23. From two Georgia Loyalists, Colonel Campbell learned that the South Carolina troops, sent into Georgia for the Florida expedition, had been withdrawn, and that Savannah was defended by less than a thousand mixed troops of Continental soldiers and Georgia militia.

The British came ashore on the morning of December 29. They were unopposed. With many times the number troops possessed by the Americans, who fled in panic, they had an easy time capturing Savannah. Colonel Campbell reported 100 Americans killed and 450 troops catpured. British losses were put at 7 dead and 19 wounded.

With the fall of the Georgia capitol, General Howe's army retreated in confusion across the Savannah River using Sister's and Zubley's ferries. During the retreat, General Howe dispatched Lieutenant Tennill with orders to Major Lane at Sunbury to evacuate his troops and join General Howe at Zubley's crossing. Instead of following orders, Major Lane was persuaded by Sunbury citizens and Captain Dollar, Commander of a company of artillery, to remain at Fort Morris. For this insubordinate action, Major Lane was later court martialed and dismissed from the service.

When word of Colonel Campbell's arrival at Tybee Island reached St. Augustine, General Augustine Prevost embarked an army of 2,000 British Regulars, Loyalists and Indians and set sail for Sunbury. His first contingent of troops landed at Colonel's Island, seven miles below Sunbury, January 6, 1779. General Prevost debarked with his light infantry and marched around behind Fort Morris to capture the town on the 7th. The main body arrived on the 8th. In spite of heavy fire from the fort, two American gallies and an armed sloop proceeded to skirt the marsh island in front of Sunbury and land mortars, cannon, and howitzers north of town.

General Prevost, next morning, sent Major Lane an ultimatum demanding surrender of the fort, unconditionally. Major Lane refused and the British guns opened up. The guns of Fort Morris replied, but it soon became evident to Major Lane that the fort could not long survive such terrific bondardment. He contacted General Prevost for better terms than unconditional surrender, but to no avail. On January 10, he surrendered Fort Morris and its garrison of seventeen officers and one hundred and ninety-five men. Twenty four pieces of artillery, ammunition and provisions fell into British hands. American losses were one captain and three privates. Seven men were wounded. The British losses were one man killed and three wounded.

Of the three American naval vessels guarding Sunbury, two gallies, the Bulloch and the Washington, were beached and burned by their crews on Ossabaw Island. The third, the armed sloop Rebecca, mounting sixteen guns, broke out and escaped to Charleston.[1]

Major Lane's reasons for not following orders to evacuate Fort Morris were given in a letter to General Howe, December 30, 1779.

"Sir,"

"About 10 o'clock this day I received your Express. I am sorry for the loss of Savannah. Your orders have forced me into a precarious Dilemma. At first I thought a retreat practicable, but when I sought among the Inhabitants for a Guide to direct

Note: [1] McCall's History of Georgia, Vol II, 1816

my rout I could not find any person equal to the task. I held a Council of War, composed of all the Officers of the Fort, and the most respectable Inhabitants, who were unanimous in opinion, that a retreat was impracticable, and that our safety was entirely dependent on a vigourous defence of the Fort. I can muster . . . . for its defence and am determined, as there is no possibility of a retreat, at all risks of my Life to defend it to the last. I feel a most poignant concern for the necessity, which urged and prompted me to defer executing immediately your Orders --- but hope it may merit a more delicate appellation when you comprehend the cause which inevitably controlled my Conduct. We have provisions sufficiently to subsist the Garrison for a considerable Siege --- and spirit, resolution and fortitude in the breast and heart of every Soldier in the Garrison to Conquer or die in case of a Storm. I hope Sir when the premises are maturely pondered by your Excellency you will not forget us, when ever you have it in your power to support us. I write the Sentiment of the whole Garrison and humbly hope that it may appear to be a sufficient sanction for my Conduct.

 I am with much Esteem
  Your Excellency's
  obedient and humble Servant

     Jos. Lane Maj & B.
     Commanding at Sunbury."

"P.S.

Notwithstanding the Contents above written --- If your Excellency thinks you cannot succour us by a speedy reinforcement, and that we shall not derive any advantage to the State from a manly and becoming resistance, and your further advice and orders shall enforce an evacuation of the Fort, I shall (provided I have a Guide sent me for the purpose) exert every faculty to execute the contents of your Express ---- As I am totally ignorant of the Country I have no hope of making a good and safe retreat, without a skillful Guide."

Following is the list of 202 men captured by British General Prevost when Fort Morris fell, January 9, 1779. Included is a total of 157 Continental Troops and 45 Sunbury Militiamen. This list is at variance with Major Lane's summary of prisoners which totaled 204. He listed 159 Continental Troops and 45 Sunbury Militiamen.

SECOND GEORGIA C: BATTALION

FIRST LIEUTENANT
Cornelius Collins

SERJEANTS
William Baker
Thomas Brown
Jesse Parker

BOWMEN
George Smith
Patrick Howell
Archibald Worldly

PRIVATES
Edward Berry
Michael Nugent

Jacob Rairberry
Robert Hutchinson
Jacob Davis
Drury Stokes
Beverly Holt
William Smith
Peter Bromback
Gibson Sutherland
John Haris
David Childers
William Collar
Daniel Bramfield
Edward McBride
John Collins
Patrick Fraey
William Drum

Thomas Handsford
William Sagers
John Lynch
Riel Ennis
Archibald Martin
Gabriel Philips
Abraham Lumly
John McIntire
John Clayton
Lyan Pea
John Honsey
Reuben Holt
James Dial
John Price
Michael Malony
Allen Battast

SECOND COMPANY OF GEORGIA ARTILLERY

CAPTAINS
Thomas Morris
John Dollar

FIRST LIEUTENANT
Philo Henley

SERJEANTS
John Walmore
John Penchier
Samuel Boyd
Samuel Peck

Daniel Hovey
John Burch
Henry Read

DRUMMER
Thomas Bond

FIFER
William Curtis

PRIVATES
John Webb
Robert Kenny

Dominic Gerold
John Newman
William Taylor
Thomas Davis
Luke Paul
William Thomas
John Campbell
George Davis
John Wright
Saml. Harrison
William Tanner
John Finley

THIRD GEORGIA BATTALION

MAJOR
Joseph Lane

CAPTAIN
Rains Cook

FIRST LIEUTENANT
John Meanly

SECOND LIEUTENANT
Josiah Maxwell

THIRD LIEUTENANT
John Peter Wagnon

SURGEON MATE
Ebenezer Calender

JUDGE ADVOCATE
David Rees

COMMISSARY
Davis Austin

QUARTERMASTER
David Fleming

SERJEANTS
Jonathan Holden
Nathan Northington
James Hays
Benjamin Wall
David Wilson

CORPORAL
Nocholas Bond

PRIVATES
John Petillo
Michael Cogbourn
Camp Burnell
Henry Pigg
John Masters
William Harnass
Swan Saunders
James Mills
William Perdue

William Allgood
David Motley
Herbert Vines
William Tucker
John Bush
Joseph Pearson
Valentine Perry
Wiott Hunley
James Davis
Jesse Hall
Thomas Hinds
Peter Stuart
Burgess Moor
Richard York
Peter Jones
Henry Smith
Obadiah Plumley
Solomon Jones
Harris Mullen
John Rickmon
Richard Biorton
Zackariah Reed

FOURTH GEORGIA BATTALLION

SUBALTERNS	PRIVATES	
Walter Dixon	John Burnett	Richard Savage
Christopher Hillary	Daniel McGinnis	Ludrick Handgarter
James Brown	John Private	Henry Fisher
	Joseph Read	John Campbell
SERJEANT	James McDannell	Joseph Webster
Charles Millen	Thomas Dixon	James Combs

THIRD SOUTH CAROLINA BATTALLION

SECOND LIEUTENANT	Thomas Harper	James Cunningham
James Robinson	Benjamin Davis	William Thomas
RANK UNKNOWN	William Sprowle	Thomas Gready
John McMahon	Thomas Burns	Thomas Condon
Hartwell Husky	John McLean	Carter Donahoe
John Edmundson	Michael Davis	Hezekiah Davis
William Williamson	Curtis Winfield	James Hilton
Mark Hodges	Philip Miller	Benja. Campbell
George Hightown	Absalom Dean	Peter Watson
Isaac Scott	William Hunter	Benjamin Harrison

SUNBURY MILITIA COMPANY

CAPTAIN	Wm. Peacock Senr.	Roger Lawson
John Kell	Samuel Davis	Alexr. Stuart
	Thos. Dickinson	Stephen Jenkins
FIRST LIEUTENANT	John Cabbage	Jacob Vernon
George Cabbage	Adam Confey	John Glazier
	David Mott	Jeremiah Plumer
SECOND LIEUTENANT	Stafford Somersall	Edward Mahorn Senr.
William Watson	William Wallace	Richard Stevens
	Samuel Main	James Lancaster
SERJEANTS	John Gilchrist	Vincent Gray
James Hamilton	Willm. Sallat	John Howell
John Simpson	Wm. Maconchy	Francis Blackrole
	John Duker	Henry Waggoner
PRIVATES	Wm. Peacock Junr.	Jean Piriart
Matthias Lapina	Adam Gray	Jean Chanier
Jeremiah Dickinson	John Graves	Antonio Arlas
William Davis	Jacob Christopher	Antonio Vouffy
Wm. Bennet Senr.	Joseph Still	Julien Duchatcaif

After the fall of Fort Morris, the British sent the Continental officers, captured at Savannah, to Sunbury on parole. Among these was Colonel George Walton of the First Georgia militia. At Savannah, his leg had been broken by a musket ball. He was captured when he fell from his horse. Walton was considered such a prize, the British asked for a Brigadier General in exchange. None being available, he was exchanged for a Navy Captian in September 1780.

George Walton was born February 2, 1741 near Farmville, Virginia, and moved to Savannah in 1769. He was admitted to the bar in 1774. He was the third Georgia signer of the

Declaration of Independence. During his career he held nearly every high office in Georgia. He was Secretary of the Provincial Council in 1775. He was President of the Council of Safety. He was Governor from November 1779 until January 1780. After the war he served as Cheif Justice for six years and in 1795 he was appointed to fill the unexpired term of United States Senator James Jackson, who had died in office. Considering his ability and accomplishments, the British were shorted when they exchanged him for an ordinary Navy Captain.

After the capture of Sunbury, General Prevost moved his troops to Savannah for a junction with Colonel Campbell, who then moved inland. Soon all Georgia was subjugated. On March 4, 1779, British civilian government was restored, with Lieutenant Colonel Mark Prevost, brother of General Prevost, as governor. A council and slate of provincial officials were appointed, and all the 1775 British laws were proclaimed in effect again. A proclamation was issued inviting all Georgians to return to the Crown and assured them England would no longer attempt to tax her colonies.

While the British held out a carrot in one hand, to repentant citizens, she swung a stick of oppression against those who still espoused the Rebel cause. Stripped of their property, their homes looted, without enough food and clothing, they became objects of charity on an already impoverished countryside. Just as had the Loyalists fled Georgia when the war began, now it was the Whigs who must find a refuge. In a letter dated January 10, 1779, General Moultrie wrote Colonel C. C. Pinckney that thousands of destitute women, children and negroes were fleeing Georgia, not knowing where they would end. "A sad spectacle that moved the hearts of his soldiers." [1] Many of these Georgia refugees reached the mountains of North Carolina where their descendants can be found today.

So great was the exodus from Sunbury that the town never regained its peak population. The Revolutionary War marked the first step in the down hill journey of the town to eventual death, fifty years later.

After the fall of Georgia, British officials began issuing restrictive proclamations. Inhabitants were instructed to collect all arms and military equipment and to surrender these to military depots. Any person found hiding materials of war was to be punished as an enemy of the King. Trading vessels were required to dock at, and sail from, certain designated wharfs, and permits were required for incoming and outgoing cargoes.

Note: [1] Memoirs of the American Revolution & c., Vol. 1, 1802

Violations were to result in the confiscation of the goods and the punishment of the crews.

British protection was offered all citizens who would swear allegiance to the Crown. The oaths were to be administered at Savannah and three months were allowed for oath taking. Two guineas for surrender of officials such as assemblymen and committeemen. Rigid price controls were put into effect. Violators were threatened with loss of their merchandise. Only those merchants who had sworn allegiance to the Crown could engage in any business. A 100 pound fine was imposed on any merchant dealing with a Rebel. No exports could be made without a certificate stating the materials were not needed by the British troops.

In spite of stringent repression against unrepentant Whigs, resistance was not completely crushed. Small bands of Rebels under such Colonels as Few, Jones and Twiggs harrassed British outposts and garrisons, cutting off supplies. Many Rebel vessels, well armed and privately owned, moved up and down the coast raiding and capturing small British craft.

One interesting story concerns a double agent, Thomas Young, who early in the war had been hired by Georgia to secure clothing for the Georgia Battalion. Secretly, he had been hired earlier by Governor Tonyn of Florida to help supply the West Indies with produce from the South Georgia plantations. He was caught. The clothing he had secured from the Georgia Battalion was seized, and his name placed on the 1778 Georgia act of confiscation and banishment.[1]

Later, from another source, Thomas Young was found living a short distance up the Midway River from Sunbury at Belfast landing.[2] On June 4, 1779, he was entertaining a party of English officers at his home, among these was Colonel Cruger. Captain Spencer, commander of an American privateer, with a dozen members of his crew, sailed up the river at night and captured the entire party. Colonel Cruger and other British officers were held under guard until morning. After they had given Captain Spencer their paroles, they were permitted to return to Sunbury. Colonel Cruger's parole was later used to secure the release of Colonel McIntosh, former Fort Morris commander who was captured at Briar Creek.

A similar incident involving another privateer occurred the same year at Sunbury. Captain Howell, the vessel's owner,

Notes: [1] The American Revolution in Georgia, 1763-1789
[2] The Dead Towns of Georgia, 1878

entered the inlet and learned from a negro slave sent out to fish for Mr. Kitchins, Collector of the port, that a group of British officers were to dine that evening at Mr. Kitchin's home in Sunbury. Reasoning that such a gathering would consume a considerable amount of liquor, Captain Howell and several of his crew rowed silently up the river, under cover of darkness, to Mr. Kitchin's place. The entire party were captured, deep in their cups.

Among those taken was Colonel Roger Kelsall, former part owner of the Kelsall and Spalding wharf. The map of Sunbury shows he owned lot No. 24, behind the wharf, which was probably the site of his store. Records of Roger Kelsall come from three separate sources,[1] and pieced together, seem to give the following story: Kelsall, being a wharf owner and merchant, was a British Loyalist. At the outbreak of the war he fled, probably to Florida, and returned to his home in Sunbury after it fell into British hands. Somewhere along the way he became a British colonel. He must have fled again when the British abandoned Georgia in 1783. His property was seized by the State of Georgia and a tract of land belonging to him, called the Distillery tract, was given to the Sunbury Academy to be sold for revenue to operate the school.

Captain Howell, on entering Mr. Kitchin's home, recognized Colonel Kelsall as the officer that had mistreated and insulted him while he was a prisoner of war. He was about to take him out to the river for drowning, when his wife's pleadings and prayers caused a change of heart. After taking paroles from the British officers, Captain Howell and his men returned to their vessel. A parole was a written promise from the person giving it not to bear arms again until he had been duly exchanged for another prisoner of war. It was a gentleman's agreement based on honor.

Among the owners of armed American privateers were Commodore Oliver Bowen and Captains Howell, Maxwell, Pray, Hardy, Stiles, Lawson and Spencer. These and others conducted raids on coastal vessels carrying British supplies. They came ashore sometimes to help fleeing Whigs remove possession from the plantations they were leaving.

Sharp naval battles often occurred such as between two American galleys and the British brigantine Dunmore mounting twelve guns. The Dunmore sailed from Sunbury for Jamaica

Note: [1] See map of Sunbury in this volume: Also list of lot owners
The Dead Towns of Georgia, 1878
Act of Georgia Legislature, Dec. 4, 1811 (conveying confiscated Kelsall land to Sunbury Academy.)

when she was attacked crossing the St. Catherine's bar.[1] Like so many historical facts found, the record was fragmentary. The result of the battle was not given.

After the American victory over the British at Yorktown, Brigadier General Anthony Wayne was sent to Georgia as Continental Commander, in January 1782. Wayne's difficulties in his new assignment were summed up as follows: "The duty we have done in Georgia is more difficult than that imposed upon the children of Israel. They had only to make brick without straw, but we have had provision, forage, and almost every other apparatus of war to procure without money: boats, bridges, etc. to build without materials except those taken from the stump: and, what was more difficult than all, to make Whigs out of Tories. But this we have effected, and have wrested the country out of the hands of the enemy, with the exception of the town of Savannah." [2]

Taking over this last British stronghold in Georgia turned out to be the easiest of all. In April, 1782, Sir Guy Carleton replaced Clinton as British Commander in North America. His instructions were to withdraw British troops from New York, Charleston, and Savannah. Savannah was the first to be evacuated. On July 10th and 11th, the last British troops departed and the Americans took possession of the city.

Lieutenant Colonel James Jackson, at the direction of General Wayne, marched in with his troops and was given the keys to the city. For twelve more days the British troops waited on Tybee Island for transportation to Charleston. The last Loyalists, under James Brown, departed for St. Augustine, July 31. Thus ended the British occupation of Georgia.

POST WAR SUNBURY

Early in August, 1782, the Georgia Legislature convened in Savannah with Governor John Martin presiding. Courts of Justice were reestablished, measures for the rehabilitation of the State were adopted, and commissioners for the administration of confiscated estates were appointed.

The following January, 1783, the Constitutional Convention assembled, and a new slate of Georgia officials were appointed. Lyman Hall was designated Governor, George Walton, Chief Justice, Samuel Stirk, Attorney General, John Milton, Secretary

Notes: [1] The Dead Towns of Georgia, 1878
[2] The American Revolution in Georgia, 1763-1789

Today . . . looking eastward down an old Sunbury street toward the Midway River. Taken on or near King's Square.

of State, John Martin, Treasurer and Richard Call, Surveyor General.

With the coming of peace, resettlement began. Many of those who had fled during the war years, returned to their old homes or began building new ones. The men released from the militia added numbers to the new land movement.

On November 18, 1783, the first session of the Supreme Court of Liberty County was held at Sunbury. Presiding was Chief Justice George Walton. Members of the Grand Jury were Joseph Law, William Baker, Sr., William Baker, Jr., James Maxwell, Palmer Goulding, John Mitchell, Jr., James Jefferies, William Quarterman, Joseph Way, Edward Way, William Way, John Winn, Jack Elliot, John Whitehead, Thomas Bradford, William West, William Peacock, Sr., John Hardy, Nathan Taylor, Nathaniel Sexton, James Powell, and John Myers, Sr.

In his charge to the jury, Chief Justice Walton began by saying that good order had characterized every court he had presided over on this, his first riding since the war ended. He assured the jury nothing could contribute more to the blessings of peace, and the general happiness of the people, than observance of the law.

He continued, "I congratulate you, gentlemen, on the news of a definitive treaty of peace by which our freedom, sovereignty and independence are secured. The war which produced it was one of necessity on our part. That we were enabled to prosecute it with firmness and perseverance to so glorious an issue should be ascribed to the protecting influence of the Great Disposer of events, and be subject of greatful praise and adoration. While the result of the contest is so honourable and advantageous to us and to posterity, it is to be lamented that those moral and religious duties so essential to the order of society and the permanent happiness of mankind, have been too much neglected. To recover them into practice, the life and conduct of every good man should be a constant example. Your temples which the profane instruments of a tyrant laid in ashes should be built again: for nothing tends to harmonize the rude and unlearned organs in man more than frequent meetings in the places of holy worship.

In the course of the conflict with an enemy whose conduct was generally marked with cruelty, the whole State has suffered undoubtedly more than any in the Confederacy. The citizens of Liberty County, with others, have drunk deep in the stream of distress. Remembering these things, we should not lose sight of the value of the prize we have obtained. And now that we are in full possession of our freedom, we should all unite in our endeavors to benefit and perpetuate the system, that we may always be happy at home and forever freed from the insults of petty tyrants commissioned from abroad."[1]

On February 26, 1784, an act was approved designating Sunbury as the place where the Superior and Inferior Courts of Liberty County were to meet. They were held here until 1797 when Riceboro was made the County Seat. [2] In 1837, the County Seat was moved again to Hinesville.

That lawlessness was a problem immediately after the Revolution can be seen from the following order signed by Governor John Martin and taken from "The Revolutionary Records of Georgia, Volume II."

MINTUES OF THE EXECUTIVE COUNCIL
Savannah   In Council 22nd October 1782.

Present
His Honor the Governor (John Martin)

Edward Jones	Thomas Maxwell	
William Glascock	Lemuel Lanier	
Jonathan Bryan		Esqs.

Notes:
[1] White's Historical Collections of Georgia 1855
[2] Watkin's Digest

WHEREAS, there are a number of notorious characters, who infest the roads and other parts in this State, and are continually murdering and plundering the virtuous inhabitants of the same, and in order to the more effectually expelling and totally annihilating those enemies to mankind (those hellish and diabolical fiends) from the face of the earth. Therefore,

ORDERED That any person either employed in the public service or otherways, shall not only be released from his term of enlistment, but shall also recieve the sum of ten guineas as a reward on his producing to the Governor and Council in Savannah the body, or good and sufficient proof that such of the under mentioned persons are absolutely and bona fide killed—

1	Samuel Moore	10	Capt. Maler.
2	George Cooke	11	William Langham
3	Henry Cooper Jun[r]	12	John Jarvis
4	William Cooper	13	John Webster
5	Samuel Cooper	14	Joseph Adams
6	Henry Cooper Sen[r]	15	Swearing Jones
7	Noah Harrill	16	Philip Thomas
8	Cudd Mobly.	17	James Altman
9	Ludd Mobly		

The health of Georgia residents was of governmental concern. This is evident by the Minutes of the Executive Council meeting, found in "The Revolutionary Records of Georgia, Volume II."

MINUTES OF THE EXECUTIVE COUNCIL

In Council, Wednesday 19th May 1784.

Present,

His Honor the Governor (Lyman Hall)

William Stephens   Jenkin Davis
John Fulton   Benjamin Andrew   Esquires

ORDERED, That the 6th 7th and part of the 9th Sections of an act of Assembly passed 26th March 1767, entitled "an act to prevent the bringing into and spreading of malignant and contagious distempers &c. &c" also the 1st and 2d Sections of another act passed the 10th May 1770, for amending the said first mentioned act, be published in the Gazette; the said acts having been revived and continued by a late act of Assembly passed 30th, July 1783.

ORDERED, pursuant to the 4th Section of the act aforesaid passed 26th March 1767, that upon the Master or Commander of any Ship or Vessel going to the Custom House of Savannah or Sunbury to enter, the Collector of the said port, do administer an oath or affirmation to such Master or Commander to make a true answer to all such questions as shall be asked him touching the health of his crew; and that thereafter the said Collector do ask the following questions of such Master or Commander, to wit, whether the place from whence the Vessel came last was healthy? Whether all the persons, passengers included, then on board such vessel, are in health and free from the small-pox, malignant fever, and all other contagious distempers? Whether any died during the voyage? of what distempers; and how long since? And that upon the said questions being answered, the said Collector do, according to circumstances, either admit such ship or vessel to an entry, and permit her to land her cargo, or otherwise act in the premises according to the directions of the said law.

POSTAL SERVICE

In early America, the postal service was the only means of communications. The arrival of the mail at the post office was a big occasion for which the town folks gathered. Letters were opened immediately and read aloud to those assembled. Newspapers were read aloud by the postmaster or the recipients. Later, both were passed from house to house.

The early mail coaches were impressive sights as can be seen from the official painting instructions issued in Washington, D. C. by Postmaster General Habersham in 1799. "The body painted green, colors formed of Prussian blue and yellow ochre; carriage and wheels red, lead mixed to approach vermillion as near as may be; octagon panel in the back, black; octagon blends green; elbow piece on rail, front rail and back, red as above; on all doors, Roman capitals in patent yellow, 'United States Mail Stage' and over these words a spread Eagle of size and color to suit."

Along the arterial roads these wonderfully painted coaches moved mail from village to village. Post offices off the main highways were serviced by lone riders on horseback. How the mail reached Sunbury is a matter of conjecture. It is believed it came by small boat from Savannah, and was moved inland by mail coach and horseback rider.

Just when the first post office was established at Sunbury is not known. Information in the National Archives and Records Service in Washington, D. C. show that the first postmaster to submit a report to Washington was Henry Schmidt on August 10, 1793. Other postmasters must have preceded him without submitting formal reports.

Following Henry Schmidt, the next Sunbury postmaster to submit a report to Washington was John Dollar on July 1, 1797. Then Mydeet Van Yeversen, April 1, 1798, James Holmes, April 1, 1801, Steven S. Wing, July 1, 1806 and Thomas Helme, October 1, 1809.

The exact date of appointment as postmaster is given for Davis Carter, February 14, 1811, Truman R. Whiteville, December 10, 1819, Paul D. Hathaway, March 26, 1828, Robert W. Law, February 25, 1829, Oliver Stevens, March 26, 1830 and Oliver W. Stevens, December 11, 1839.

The post office at Sunbury was discontinued April 24, 1841.

THE SUNBURY ROAD

The Sunbury Road was the longest vehicular road in early post-Revolutionary Georgia. It skirted the frontier, beginning in the Piedmont Uplands at Greensboro and ending in the Lower Coastal Plains at Sunbury. It followed a remarkably elevated route with few stream crossings as it passed through prosperous farm lands, poor sandy locations and virgin pine woods. The largest stream crossed was Canoochee Creek at Taylors Creek Crossroads in Liberty County roughly eighteen miles from the old Midway Church. It is believed that either a bridge or a ferry served here from earliest times since this was a fairly well-settled locality.

Dr. John H. Goff of Emory University, writing in the "Georgia Mineral Newsletter," Volume VIII, Number 3, Autumn 1955, states. "The first formal step to provide Sunbury with an arterial road deep into the interior came in 1786 when the General Assembly enacted a law which called for the laying out of a route from Sunbury to Washington in Wilkes County. This project was not carried through. One is not certain of what happened but it is suspected the interests of other centers blocked the move, since the act was noted as unnecessary on

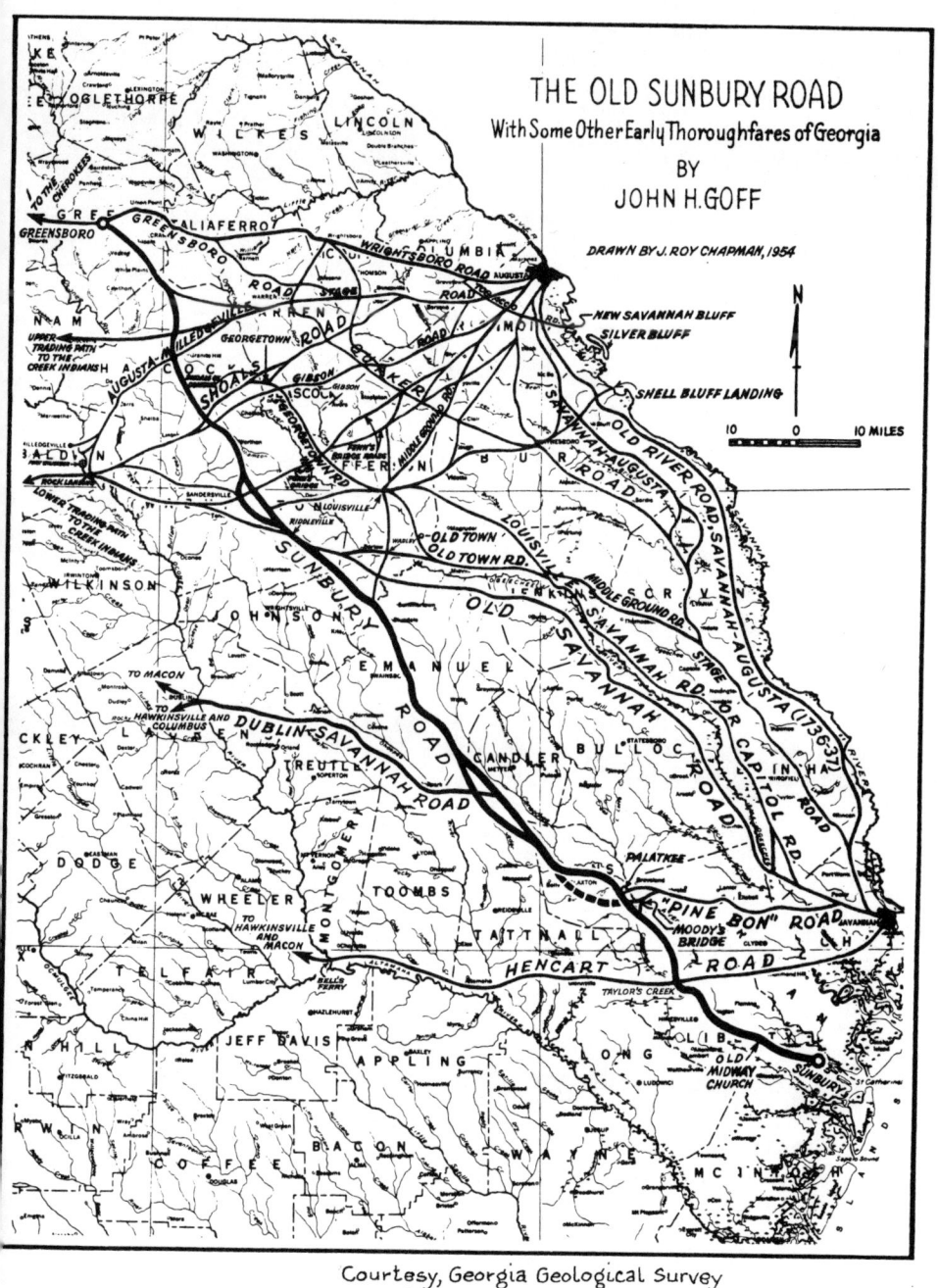

Courtesy, Georgia Geological Survey
Georgia Mineral Newsletter, vol. VIII, No. 3, Autumn 1955

the basis that the power for establishing and altering public roads had already been vested by law in the courts of the several counties."

In the immediately ensuing years after this act little information is available about a road from Sunbury to the hinderland. One concludes though that her people were busy "lining up friends" for a route because an act dated December 1792 mentions a road that "hath been laid out" from Green County Court House (today's Greensboro) to Liberty County. Apparently the Sunbury and Liberty County interests working from the coastal end had persuaded road authorities of the frontier counties involved to cooperate in the opening and linking a major route in their direction. The thoroughfare was actually in use prior to the time it was mentioned in the act since some Washington County land plats dated in May 1792 show and name Sunbury Road. The beginning of the route at Greensboro was further confirmed in 1797 when another act again mentions the road as leading from the court house in Green County to the town of Sunbury.

This route then dating from the early 1790's became the Sunbury Road. The accompanying map depicts the course of the old way and shows some of its connections. It also gives certain other important early thoroughfares of Georgia, among which are the competitive roads that led from Augusta and Savannah into territory traversed by the way from Sunbury."

The town of Sunbury was incorporated by a legislative act, December 8, 1791. The second Monday in January, 1792, and every three years thereafter, elections were to be held for Commissioners. To vote, a person had to be an adult male and the owner of a house or lot. Eligible voters were to meet where the courts were held, and under the supervision of two Justices of the Peace of Liberty County, were to vote for five of their qualified citizens for Commissioners.

Following the election, the Commissioners were to meet and appoint their own officers and clerk. The Commissioners had the power to make regulations, impose penalties, raise taxes and provide law and order. Each year the Commissioners were to assess every person who "shall inhabit, hold, use, occupy or possess or enjoy any lot, ground, house, building, tenement, or hereitament within the town of Sunbury, for raising such sum or sums of money as the said Commissioners or a majority of them shall judge necessary for and towards carrying this Act into execution; and in case of a refusal or neglect to pay such

This is the old wharf area of Sunbury. The marshy island in the background divides the Midway River.

rate or assessment, the same shall be levied and recovered by warrant of distress and sale of the offenders goods, under the hand and seals of the said Commissioners or a majority of them, or under the hand and seal of any Justice of the Peace for the County of Liberty."[1] The Commissioners were also appointed superintendents of pilotage for the port of Sunbury, and given the authority of Justices to maintain law and order.

The commissioners continued to run the town government until about 1825, when the elections went by default. By this time, Sunbury no longer had enough citizens to need central government. Each person was entrusted to look after his own property and to cooperate with his few neighbors in cutting the weeds. Cows roamed at will. Gradually the Bermuda grass took possession of the vacant lots, streets, lanes and squares.

Although the war with England had ended, trouble with the Indians continued to be a problem to the people of Liberty County. A man was scalped eighteen miles from Sunbury on October 24, 1787. Three others were killed and their scalps taken within the Midway settlement, January 9, 1788. Two skirmishes against the Indians occurred at Pinholloway Creek and at Shepards plantation. Mr. Girardeau's plantation was attacked on May 1, and several of his slaves taken captives. One slave was injured resisting the Indians.

Note: [1] Watkins' Digest

Colonel Maybank's place was also attacked and several of his negroes abducted. A young man milking a cow was killed in a raid at Sapelo. The plantation of the former Georgia governor, John Houstoun, was attacked on June 6, and a man named McCormick was killed, his son scalped, and another smaller son and three daughters taken captives. A raid on Mr. Quarterman's plantation resulted in the loss of thirteen slaves taken captive. However, militia men overtook the Indians at Taylor's Creek and they fled leaving the slaves behind.[1]

To meet the Indian menace, the people of Liberty county at their own expense in September 1788 raised a company of horsemen commanded by Captain Rudolph, two other officers, two sergeants, and forty privates whose main duty was scouting. Citizens carried arms wherever they went even to church on Sunday. This defensive posture continued until the Treaty of Colerain was signed with the Indians.

Education was greatly encouraged in postwar Georgia. The constitution of 1777 provided that "schools shall be erected in each county, and supported at general expense of the state." While the war lasted nothing was done to implement the act, but, in 1783, Governor Lyman Hall in his message to the assembly recommended that steps be taken to encourage both education and religion. He recommended that lands be granted to endow schools. The Richmond Academy, the first public school in Georgia, opened in Augusta in April 1785.

In Liberty County, the Sunbury Academy was established by law in February 1788 with 1000 pounds worth of confiscated estates being set aside for its support. It was an excellent school and for many years the most famous in South Georgia. Students were drawn from many counties in the state and even some from other states were attracted. A governing body of five commissioners was named to administer the school. One of these was Abiel Holmes, the father of the author, Oliver Wendell Holmes and grandfather of the Chief Justice of the United States Supreme Court by the same name. The other four were Peter Winn, John Elliot, Gideon Dowse and James Dunwoody.

The Sunbury Academy was coeducational. Art, mathematics, civil engineering, navigation, Greek, Latin and English were taught. Graduates were accepted as juniors at Yale, Harvard and Princeton where a great many went to continue their education.

The Commissioners were given authority to sell at public auction any confiscated property in Liberty County up to the

Note: [1] White's Historical Collections of Georgia, 1855

amount of 1,000 pounds value. The money to be used for building the Academy, which was constructed in King's Square. It was a wooden structure, two and a half stories high and about sixty feet square.

Teachers employed at the Sunbury academy were Rev. Dr. William McWhir, Mr. James E. Morris, Rev. Mr. Lewis, Rev. Shannon, Rev. Thomas Goulding, Mr. Uriah Willcox, Rev. John Boggs, Captain William Hughes, Mr. C. G. Lee, Rev. A. T. Holmes, Rev. S. G. Hillyer, Major John Winn, Mr. W. T. Feay, and Mr. Oliver Wendell Stevens.

The last known act of the Legislature, concerning the Academy, was passed on December 4, 1811. It was a grant of one-third of a tract of land adjoining Sunbury, confiscated from the estate of Roger Kelsall.

The Principal of the Academy was the Reverend Doctor William McWhir who was also its most noted teacher, and the man most responsible for establishing and maintaining the school's high standards. He was a native of Belfast, Ireland, a graduate of Belfast college, and an ordained Presbyterian minister. He migrated to America in 1783 and located in Alexandria, Virginia where he became Principle of the Academy there. George Washington was a trustee of this school and became a good friend and admirer of Reverend McWhir.

McWhir was often a guest at Mount Vernon. It is recorded on one occasion, while dining that George Washington said the blessing himself instead of calling on the Reverend McWhir, as would normally have been the case with a minister in attendance. Surprised, Martha Washington remarked that her husband must have forgotten that a member of the clergy was present. To which General Washington replied, "I desire clergymen, as well as others, to see that I am not a graceless man."[1]

In 1793, the Reverend McWhir moved to Sunbury, to become the Principal of the Academy there. He was a scholar, learned in English, Latin and Greek, and a stern disciplinarian. To the ambitious students he was a dedicated instructor full of help and encouragement, but to the slothful he was a terror, having been trained in the old school in Ireland where the stick was as important as the book in the learning process.

He was a welcome guest at night in the homes of his former students and other learned citizens of Sunbury. He was very fond of an evening of social talk and his favorite drink was buttermilk, occasionally spiked with wine or rum for tonic.

Note: [1] The Dead Towns of Georgia, 1878

Tomb of Reverend William McWhir, Principal of the Sunbury Academy, in the abandoned Sunbury Cemetary.

After serving for 30 years at the Academy, he retired to his neighboring plantation, "Springfield," where he continued teaching as a private instructor. He never gave up preaching and served as a supply minister of the gospel along the Coast. He organized the first Presbyterian church in Florida near St. Augustine and a later one at Mandarin. McWhir died January 30, 1851. Today his grave is tilted and almost hidden in the dense undergrowth in the abandoned cemetary at Sunbury.

It is uncertain when the Academy finally closed its doors, but it is recorded the building was dismantled and sold in 1842. As late as 1829, or five years after McWhir's departure, the Academy was still in operation. An account written that year by Mr. Sherwood of the Georgia Gazette discribed Sunbury as having a flourishing academy, a house of worship for the Baptists, twenty dwelling houses, two stores, three offices, and a population of one hundred and fifty.

The Sunbury Female Asylum was incorporated by the Georgia legislature, November 23, 1819. This institution was to be supported by "generous charities of kind hearted women .... for the humane purpose of relieving, protecting and instructing orphan children of their sex." What happened after the act was passed is uncertain.

During the War of 1812, Sunbury prepared, as best she could, to meet the new English threat. Fort Morris, which had been renamed Fort George by the British after its capture, changed names again. This time it was called Fort Defense. Labor to repair the rundown fort was furnished by slaves from the local plantations. The whole area was cleaned, the walls and parapet strengthened, and the moat dug out. Old armament was cleaned and put into service. A few new light pieces of artillery were obtained from Savannah. General C. C. Pickney was requisitioned for two 18-pounders and enough ammunition to service the guns.

The Committee of Safety for Liberty County was composed of William Fleming, John Winn, Joseph Law, John Stacy, John Elliott, John Stevens, and General Daniel Stewart. General Stewart was the great-grandfather of President Theodore Roosevelt. The Committee was charged with the defense of the County and had the authority to call upon the citizens for whatever labor was needed in the defense effort.

Sunbury organized a forty man company of citizens for the town's defense under the command of John A. Cuthbert. A second company was made up of students from the Sunbury Academy and from the town teenagers. This was under the command of Captain Floyd. Beside these two companies, three other volunteer groups were formed in Liberty County. These were the Liberty Independence Troop, headed by Captain Joseph Jones, and two infantry companies commanded by Captains John Winn and Robert Quarterman.

The County militia was mainly concerned with scouting the coast area for possible British landings. However, during the entire three years the war lasted, not a single shot was fired in combat. Occasionally, smoke from a burning merchantman, caught by the British, could be seen off the Georgia coast, but no attempt was made to attack either Sunbury or Fort Defense.

However, the British did invade Georgia in January, 1815, even though the war was officially ended by treaty, December 24, 1814. News of the peace treaty signing in Europe was slow in travelling and did not reach Admiral Sir George Cockburn of the British Navy before he had landed 2,000 seasoned troops on the South Georgia coast. He captured and pillaged the town of St. Marys, plundered Jekyll Island and occupied St. Simons and Cumberland islands before withdrawing his forces when word of the war's end reached him on February 25.

The Liberty Independent Troop, second oldest volunteer military company in Georgia, annually held a gala Fourth of July celebration in Sunbury until 1833. This was a big day for the town with music, marching, rifle matches, picnics and patriotic speeches. Sometimes, a United States Revenue cutter, stationed along the coast would dock at Sunbury and its crew some ashore for the festivities.

The old Midway Church built in 1792 to replace the one burned by the British in 1778. A division of General Sherman's Army camped here in 1864 for six weeks.

In 1814, a large Swedish ship docked at Sunbury to pick up a load of cotton. This was believed to have been the last large vessel to use the port. Mr. James Holmes was the last Collector of the port whose duties were almost non-existant.

Destruction, anguish and poverty followed the Northern Army's march through Georgia in 1864. A division of General Sherman's cavalry under General Kilpatrick, camped for six weeks at Midway using the fenced cemetery for a cattle pen, the church for a commissary and the church organ for a meat block. The men of theDivision spread through Liberty County burning buildings, barns, and crops and slaughtering cattle and horses. At Sunbury they burned the Baptist Church, to signal offshore gunboats the town was in Northern hands. Hundreds of freed slaves roamed at will throughout the almost deserted county tearing down houses and using the lumber to build living quarters for themselves.

The white plantation owners, who had not already fled, found it impossible to raise rice and cotton without black labor. As many as could left to join friends and relatives, some as far away as Texas. Those who remained lived in poverty. The Midway Society held its last annual meeting in December 1865. The last inscriptions in the Church Record Book were dated in October 1867.

SUNBURY SLEEPS

Why did Sunbury die? No one really knows why one person or town will live while another person or town will die. Here are some of the reasons Sunbury did not survive.

(1) Georgia simply could not support two seaports just 28 miles apart. One or the other had to go.

(2) Sunbury's existence depended on rice production and rice exports. With the rise in the production of cotton and tobacco, rice production decreased. Improved roads made marketing to Savannah easier and more convenient than to Sunbury.

(3) Sunbury never recovered from the population loss suffered during the Revolutionary War when Loyalists and their families migrated to Florida and the Whigs north into the Carolinas.

(4) Sickness killed too many. Malaria from the rice swamps of Liberty County and epidemics of other diseases made Sunbury a health hazard. In the late 1850's an epidemic of yellow fever struck. The homes of the victims were burned in an effort to stop the disease.[1]

(5) The great hurricanes of 1804 and 1824 tore down houses and docks and killed some people in exposed places. This made many people fearful of living so close to sea.[2]

No matter what caused the death of Sunbury its influence in America's birth will be remembered. It was Sunbury and St. Johns Parish, renamed Liberty County in 1777, that furnished the revolutionary spark necessary for Georgia to join the other twelve colonies in the Revolutionary War.

In "The Dead Towns of Georgia", C. C. Jones, whose ancestors came from Liberty County, wrote the following nostalgic epitaph for Sunbury in 1878:

"Without trade, destitute of communications, and visited more and more each season with fevers, Sunbury, for nearly thirty years has ceased to exist save in name. Its squares, lots, streets and lanes have been converted into a corn field. Even the brick of the ancient chimneys have been carried away. No sails whiten the blue waters of Midway river save those of a miserable little craft employed by its owners in conveying

Notes:
[1] Georgia, Land of the Golden Isles, 1956
[2] Georgia Mineral Newsletter, Vol. VIII No. 3., 1955

terrapins to Savannah. The old cemetery is so overgrown with trees and brambles that the graves of the dead can scarcely be located after the most diligent search. Fort Morris is enveloped in a wild growth of cedars and myrtle. Academy, churches, markets, billiard rooms, wharves, storehouses, residences, all gone: only the bold Bermuda covered bluff and the beautiful river with the green island slumbering in its embrace remain to remind us of this lost town.

A stranger pausing here would find no trace of the past once full of life and importance, but now existent only in the skeleton memories which redeem place and name from oblivion which sooner or later is the common lot of all things human. The same bold bluff, — the same broad expanse of marshes stretching onward to the confines of the broad Atlantic, — the same blue outline of Colonel's Island and the Bryan shore, — the same sea-washed beaches of St. Catherine, — the same green islands dividing the river as it ebbs and flows with ever restless tide, — the same soft breezes, — the same bright skies, — the same sweet voices and tranquil scene which nature gave and still perpetuates, — but all else how changed! Truly "oblivion is not to be hired." Blindly scattering her poppy she deals with places as with men, and they become as though they had not been. Strange that a town of such repute, and within the confines of a young and prosperous commonwealth, should have so utterly faded from the face of the earth."

> "The garden with its arbor — gone,
> And gone the orchard green;
> A shattered chimney stands alone,
> Possessor of the scene."

Almost a hundred years later, 1975 this description is still accurate. Today there is only a small restaurant and dock catering to fishermen, a few neat houses, many historical markers, the ruins of Fort Morris, now undergoing restoration, and the abandoned old cemetery. Everywhere else a grey fog of forgetfullness covers the dead town of Sunbury, Georgia.

1775 map section showing Dorchester in the center

THE DEAD TOWN OF DORCHESTER

On the north bank of the Ashley River, eighteen miles northwest of Charleston, South Carolina, and six miles southwest of Summerville, lies the ruins of the dead town of Dorchester. It was founded in 1696 by members of the Congregational Church from the Puritan colony at Dorchester, Massachusetts sent south to establish a church community. Today nothing remains of this once flourishing settlement but a part of the entrance gate, the bell tower of the old Anglican church, and the sturdy walls of old Fort Dorchester, which played an important part in the American Revolution.

The story of old Dorchester, once the third largest town in South Carolina, had its beginning in England during the Puritan Revolution. In 1620 a group of Puritans from the counties of

69

Dorcet, Somerset, and Devon came together at Plymouth, England. Their purpose was to form a colony and migrate to the New World. They were brought together by the Rev. John White. Although he did not accompany them, he had expressed a deep interest in their undertaking. One hundred and forty Puritans made up the group. After a day of fasting and prayer, they put out to sea, March 30, 1630, in a 400 ton vessel named "Mary and John." It was commanded by Captain Squeb.

On May 30th, they entered the harbor of Nantasket, Massachusetts. Several search parties were sent out to explore before it was decided to land at Matapan. During the summer they began building their town which they named Dorchester after the town in England from which many had come.

In 1635, a large group of members became dissatisfied with Dorchester and moved to what is now Windsor, Connecticut. They were accompanied by their minister, Rev. John Warham. Their other minister, Rev. John Maverick died unexpectedly in Boston, February 3, 1636, while preparing to make the journey to rejoin the group. The population gap at Dorchester was soon filled by other Puritans arriving from England. Rev. Richard Mather brought a group when he arrived.

The Church of England was predominant in South Carolina, but in 1695, there were many settlers living on grants outside of Charleston with protestant learnings. These Puritans were desirous of establishing an independent church of their own in their locality. Therefore, it was decided to send a request to the Dorchester, Massachusetts colony to send a Congregational minister to organize a church. William Norman, holder of a 320 acre grant was selected to personally carry the message.

In Dorchester, William Norman's petition was favorably received. Mr. Joseph Lord, who was shortly to be ordained, was selected to lead a group of churchmen to establish the church in South Carolina. In the "Records of the First Church at Dorchester, New England," the event is covered thusly:

"October 22, 1695, being lecture day, was set apart for the ordination of Mr. Joseph Lord, to go to South Carolina, to settle the gospel there, and the names of the men (to accompany him) are these: Joshua Brooks, Simon Draken and Nathaniel Billings of Concord; William Norman of Carolina; William Adams of Sudbury; George Fox of Reading and Increase Sumner and William Pratt of Dorchester."

"These, with Mr. Lord, did enter into a most solemn covenant to set up the ordinances of Jesus Christ there, if the Lord carried them safely thither (according to the gospel truth, with a very large profession of their faith.)"

About six weeks after the ordination of Rev. Lord, the little group sailed from Boston harbor in the brigantine "Friendship," commanded by Captain Hill. The following account is from the church records:

"December 5, 1695, the church of South Carolina set sail from Boston. On December 14th, at night, the skiff was near run under water, the stormy wind being so boisterous. They kept a day of prayer on board and landed safely at Carolina, December 20th."

On arrival at Charleston the brigantine with its church members was given a nine gun salute, and warmly welcomed by the townspeople. There they spent several weeks examining different locations before deciding to settle the colony on the Ashley River, just below the plantation of William Norman. The river was navigable by small craft all the way to Charleston from this point.

The land was low and swampy, but dotted with fertile hammocks that were easily cultivated. Rice was the chief money crop of the Province, and since rice required a swampy environment to grow, this location seemed ideal. At the time of settlement most of the country was in a state of wild forest with the exception of the plantations nearby. Indians were not far away.

The town of Dorchester was laid out on a 50 acre tract and was to serve as a market center for the community. It was part of an 1,800 acre tract granted to John Smith, November 20, 1696. The tract was known as "Boo-shoo," an Indian name, the meaning of which has been lost. The Smith family were of considerable means. John Smith was a member of the South Carolina Grand Council. Sometime before 1682 he must have died because the record shows his wife remarried Arthur Middleman in December, 1682. For reasons unknown, the Smith grant reverted to the State. On July 7, 1696, the 1,800 acre tract was regranted to John Stevens, along with another 2,200 acre called "Roseland." The two grants totaled 4,050 acres and were to be used for "the benefit of the intending settlers of the Church." Together they comprised the Township of Dorchester.

The 50 acre market town of Dorchester was laid out on a bluff on the northeast side of the Ashley river in an open field previously cleared by John Smith. It possibly contained his old homestead. The town was divided by streets running northeast

Plan for Town of DORCHESTER, S. C.

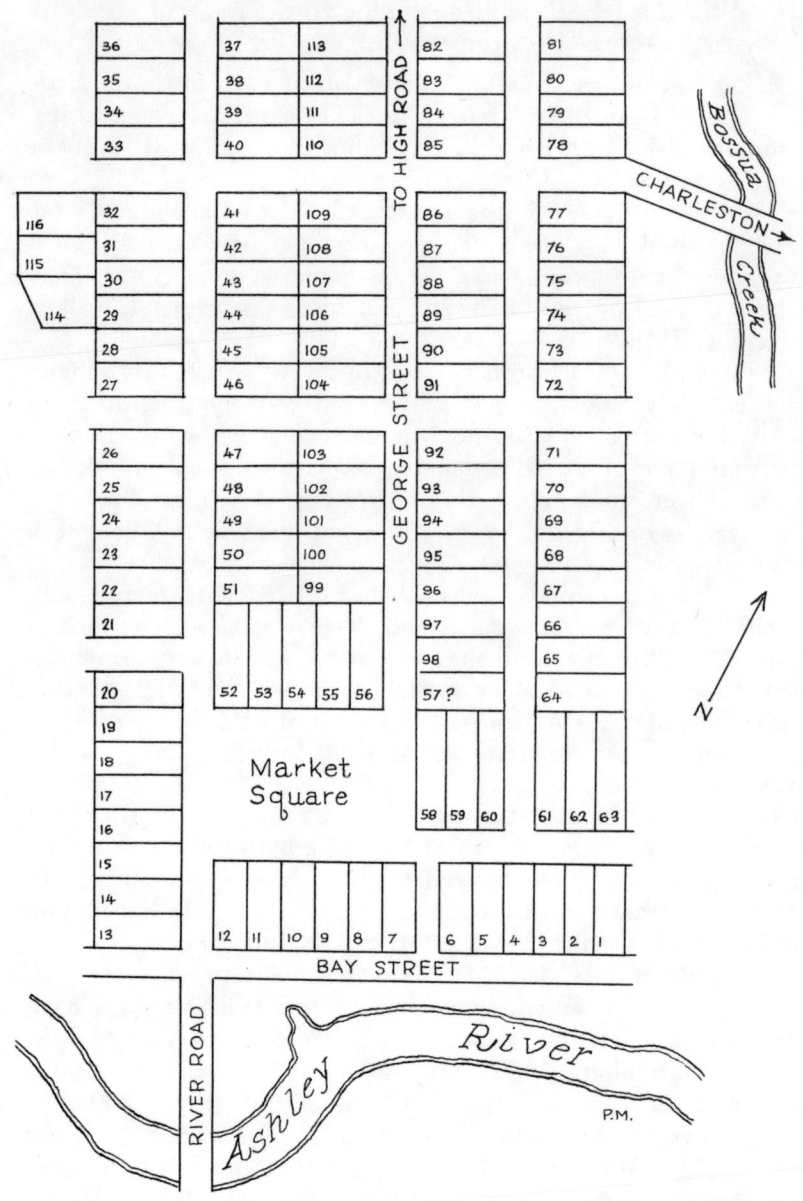

and southwest at right angles. Each lot contained a quarter of an acre. There were 116 lots, and a public square, or market place, over an acre in size.

East of town, along Dorchester Creek, a 20 acre tract was set aside for public use. West of town, another 52 acre tract was designated public land. North of town, 123 acres of "mill land" was for the community use.

The remaining land of the 4,050 acres comprising the Township of Dorchester was divided into two divisions of two ranges each. The first range of the first division contained 26 lots of 50 acres each. Lot No. 1 began about three and one half miles west of town at the William Norman boundary and numbered down, with Lot. No. 26 adjoining the town commons. Facing the Ashley River each lot was 10 chains (660 feet) wide and 50 chains (3,300 feet) deep.

The second range of the first division was north of the first range and was separated from it by a roadway. It contained 26 lots of 45 acres each. Immediately north of the second range and separated from it by another roadway was the second division. All lots in this division were also 45 acres. The eastern part of the town of Summerville, from about Fourth South Street on the north and Sumter Avenue on the west was part of the second division which was taken out of the "Roseland" grant.

There is no known list of the original lot owners. However, from data contained in subsequent land transfers, wills, and conveyances, the following partial list was derived: Rev. Joseph Lord, John Stevens, Increase Sumner, Samuel Sumner, William Pratt, William Adams, Micheal Bacon, John Simmons, Abraham Gordon, Jonathan Clarke, Thomas Osgood, Job Champerlain, Arron Way, Sr., Aaron Way, Jr., William Way, Samuel Way and Robert Miller.

Later land records show the following men purchased lots: David Batchelor in 1707, Issac Brunson, 1712, Robert Winn, 1718, John Kitchen and Thomas Graves, 1722, Thomas Satur, 1722, John Hill, 1726, Steven Dowse, 1727, and Peter Savey, 1738.

The countryside bordering the Township of Dorchester seems to have been pretty well settled. Lord Shaftesbury's barony lay to the south, on the opposite side of the Ashley River. Colonel Andrew Percival's plantation, granted in 1682, was to the west. The William Norman tract, granted in 1684, was northwest. East, along the Ashley River, nearly all the land had been granted. There was another settlement about six miles away on Goose Creek.

The early history of Dorchester is scanty. Its strategic location, at the head of the Ashley River, made it a trading center and a shipping point to the interior. Located between the

73

Ashley River and Dorchester Creek, it was easy to defend, and was considered a point of refuge in case of an Indian uprising.

As Dorchester prospered, merchants secured lots in the town and set up businesses. By 1717, there were 1,800 inhabitants. Only two street names have survived. Bay Street, which ran parallel to the Ashley River, and George Street which joined the public road leading into town. In 1722, Thomas Satur of Dorchester, Jacob Satur of London, Eleazer Allen and William Rhett of Charleston formed a co-partnership. Their business was not given. In 1724, Gillison Clapp, business unknown, was listed as a merchant on Bay Street.

From a June 1, 1742 map of Dorchester, the last names of the following men were given as lot owners: Roughman, Vanverloon, Fisher, Moody, Davidson, Roberts, Baker, Waring, Middleton, Blake, Simonds, Chastinger, Benit & Gordon, Cattel, Stone, Waring, Way, Stevens, Blake and Holmes. This was not a complete list as the note below the map stated, "Plan of the town of Dorchester with the names of some of the owners at present inserted."[1]

An Act passed in 1723 provided for a market and semiannual fairs in the town of Dorchester, "it being a frontier in that part of the Country." As the frontier expanded, roads were extended by statute into the surrounding country. Steven's bridge and Waring's bridge over the Ashley River were made public property. Navigation of the Ashley was improved by dredging.

THE DORCHESTER FREE SCHOOL

In 1724, an Act was passed for founding a free school in Dorchester. The Act was the result of petition sent to the Crown in England. The plea stated in general, that due to the blessing of the Almighty God, the youths of the Providence had become numerous and that the parents were desirous of having them instructed in grammar, liberal arts, sciences, and in the principles of Christian living. No immediate action seems to have been taken to get the school going.

In 1734, another Act was passed appointing twelve commissioners to implement the establishment of the Dorchester school. The commissioners were: Rev. Francis Varod, Thomas Skene, John Williams, Thomas Waring, Joseph Blake, Arthur Middleton, Robert Wright, Ralph Izard, Walter Izard, Paul Jenys, Benjamin Waring and William Cattell. There is no record that this commission accomplished anything in spite of the

Note: [1] History & Records of Midway Church

community's need for education. It is possible that the Congregational Church conducted its own school teaching and objected to a free school. This is speculation based on the fact that in 1756, after the Congregationalist moved in mass to Georgia, a third Act was passed naming a new commission, and this time the school was started.

Members of the 1756 commissioners were Henry Middleton, Walter Izard, Ralph Izard, Benjamin Waring, Richard Waring, Joseph Waring, Daniel Blake and the Rev. Langhorne, rector of St. George's Church.

All members of this commission were influential citizens and they immediately set about building the school. The minutes of Free School, March, 1758, state that two brick houses, 23 feet wide by 36 long, each one story high, with Dutch type roofs, were ordered built. One building was to serve as the school house and the other the home of the school master.

To obtain the services of a teacher, an advertisement was placed in England. Where this advertisement was placed was not given. The requirements specified a male teacher capable of teaching the languages, some branches of mathematics, and having a tolerable good hand. Salary was to be 800 pounds sterling on condition that he stay for two years. An additional 400 pounds sterling would be given to cover passage from England to South Carolina.

The advertisement seems to have attracted no takers deemed satisfactory. The Free School records indicate that several years passed before the Rev. John Allison was hired. Where he came from and the exact year he was hired were not given. Obviously he was highly educated, as the subjects he taught were reading, writing, arithmatic, geography, astronomy, orthography elocution, English, Latin and Greek.

The Dorchester Free School name is puzzling since the pupils were required to pay tuition. However, each year ten pupils from financially needy homes were admitted free of charge.

Several wealthy citizens made generous donations to the school. Among these were Samuel Wragg, who gave 100 pounds, Daniel Blake, 300 pounds, and Peter Taylor, 500 pounds. The school flourished.

During the Revolutionary War, the British damaged the school, but it was later repaired and used. However, by this time, Dorchester had lost most of its population and the need for the school became doubtful. In 1814, the commissioners began looking for another location. An 1817 Act ratified its movement and it was relocated in Summerville.

The Dorchester school property was sold and the funds were used to help build the new school on a 40 acre plot of land donated by James R. Stewart.

THE WHITE MEETING HOUSE

The White Meeting House, or Congregational Church, was built in 1696 and was located about two miles above town on the east side of the public road. This was a wooden structure and it was replaced by a brick building in 1700. There are two theories about how the church received its name. One theory holds it was named in honor of the Rev. John White, the Puritan colony organizer in England. The other theory holds it was so named because of the white plaster used to cover the brick building built in 1700. It is interesting to note that the descendents of this colony, when they migrated to Georgia in 1752, named their first church there the White Meeting House. It was burned by the British in 1778.

The Dorchester church was built on Lot No. 9 in the first range of the first division. Lot No. 10 was later donated by the Rev. Joseph Lord, thus making 100 acres available.

It has been claimed and disputed that the first Holy Communion ever held in South Carolina was conducted at Dorchester, under the branches of an oak tree, at the future site of the White Meeting House, by the Rev. Joseph Lord. From the "Records of the First Church at Dorchester, New England," the following account was recorded:

"February 2, 1696. The first Sacrament of the Lord's Supper that was ever celebrated in Carolina. Eight persons received besides such as were of the Church by virtue of Communion of Churches, and there was great joy among the good people of Carolina and many thanksgivings to the Lord."

Since this entry was recorded second hand after the event by the church recorder in Dorchester, New England, it must be assumed that neither he nor the bearer of the record were aware of South Carolina church history. Those who dispute the entry point out that for many years prior, in Charleston, there existed an Anglican Church, a Congregational Church and a Huguenot, or French Protestant Church. Certainly these churches celebrated communion after their own rituals, long before the Dorchester communion.

By the year 1737, the membership of the White Meeting House had so expanded, it was felt necessary to build another branch at Beach Hill. It was constructed of wood on a 95 acre tract of land on the Beach Hill road near the St. Paul's Parish line. One minister served both churches.

Between 1752 and 1756, nearly the entire membership of the Dorchester and Beech Hill churches migrated to Georgia. Services at Beech Hill were discontinued and the church building soon fell into disrepair and was abandoned. The White Meeting House was used intermittently for many years, even though it had no resident minister. The remaining members entered into an agreement with the Presbyterian Church to supply ministers from time to time.

During the Revolutionary War, the British set fire to the Dorchester Church which destroyed the interior. The brick walls remained standing. In 1794, the church was reorganized and repaired. By 1815, the last resident minister had departed. The parsonage house and the church land were sold. By this time the remaining members had transferred to the Presbyterian Church in Summerville. In 1882, the church was abandoned and in decay. In 1886, the Charleston earthquake collapsed the building, leaving only one wall standing. Today, this crumbling wall and the church graveyard are all that remain of the old White Meeting House.

The bell tower is all that remains of the Anglican church.

ST. GEORGE'S ANGLICAN CHURCH

In 1706, an Act was passed establishing the Church of England the State Church of South Carolina. At this time the Province contained six parishes. Dorchester was located in St. Andrew's. In 1719, St. Andrew's Parish was divided into two parts. The upper part became St. George's Parish and contained Dorchester and its surroundings.

Although Dorchester had been founded by Congregationalists, many of the people residing in the town and in St. George's Parish belonged to the Church of England. In 1719, a statute was passed providing for the construction of an Anglican Church in St. George's Parish. The South Carolina General Assembly appointed a commission to select a church site and to raise part of the money for constructing the building. The commission members were: John Cantey, Walter Izard, Thomas Diston, Samuel Wragg, Thomas Waring and Jacob Satur.

The Statute appropriated 334 pounds toward the project. The commissioners raised another 1,196 pounds by subscription. Later a final 466 pounds was added by the General Assembly. Dorchester was selected for the church site and Lots 52, 53, 54, 55 and 56 were purchased. The church property faced on the Public Square. Another 150 acres were secured for the church glebe outside of town. Its exact location is not known. In 1734, it was decided the church glebe and parsonage house were too far from the church, so the 150 acre tract was sold. A smaller tract of 75 acres was secured closer to town. Lot No. 25 in the first range of the first division contained 50 acres of this plot. Another 25 acres, or half a lot, was added. The lot number was not given.

Church construction began in 1719 and was completed in 1720. The building was brick, 30 feet wide and 50 feet long, exclusive of the chancel, the dimensions of which were not given.

In 1734, an Act was passed stating that the church was in poor condition and was too small for the congregation. It directed the wardens to make repairs, add more pews, and construct a church addition. This addition must have been the bell tower. In 1739 Parliment appropriated 300 pounds for the parsonage. No details were given.

In 1752, the parishioners enlarged the parsonage, added an outhouse and bought two slaves to serve the rector. A handsome steeple was added to the church building, and a subscription was begun to buy bells for the bell tower.

During the Revolutionary War, the church was damaged by the British and left in a ruinous condition. In 1811, it was repaired and divine services again held there for a short time. However, by now, Dorchester was a nearly deserted village. The few remaining members of the congregation moved their affiliations to the functioning Anglican church in St. Paul's Parish, six miles away.

In 1820, Dr. Dalcho, historian of the Church Dioceses, wrote that the St. George's Parish Church was in a ruinous state, without a rector, and that its records were lost. Some years later it was devastated by fire of uncertain origin, and the interior and roof destroyed. In time, vandals removed the brick from the wall and foundations for buildings in Summerville. Today, all that remains of the old Anglican Church is the bell tower and a few scattered tombstones in the graveyard.

FORT DORCHESTER

The best preserved ruins in Dorchester today are of the old fort facing the Ashley River. Just when it was built is not clear. A State sign before the fort gives 1757 as the date of construction. However, the December 1875 issue of "Harper's New Monthly Magazine," gives a much earlier date for its construction. The article says, in part:

"Here on the Ashley is a well preserved fortification, a deserving remembrance now, if ever. Its walls are tabby, from eight to ten feet high; the enclosed ground within is covered with a thick growth of forest trees; in the center is a mound, covering the debris of the magazine; cedars of venerable aspect

Today, the coquina walls of Fort Dorchester are still standing.

line its outer face, and in some places have fallen across; but the old walls stand firmly, and the broad top is solid and even."

"It is known that this fort was built before 1719, as a protection against the Indians, and probably it dates even farther back. It was repaired in 1775 as a place of refuge in case Charleston should be captured and was used as a gathering point for the militia and for covering the back country."

When the fort was built is an open question. However, it is certain some kind of fortification was built shortly after the founding of Dorchester in 1696 because of the Indian menace. A wooden stockade or blockhouse must have preceded the tabby fort to protect this frontier settlement.

THE REVOLUTIONARY WAR

In July, 1775, the Safety Council directed a survey and fortification of Fort Dorchester. In October, 1775 part of the public store of powder and ordinance, along with the public records, were moved into the fort for safekeeping. In November, 1775, Capt Francis Marion, commanding two companies of soldiers, was garrisoned there. This action was recorded in General Moultrie's Memoirs thusly:

"November, 1775. Information having been received that the Scoffol Light Troops were coming down from the back country in great force to carry off the ammunition and public records that were lodged at Dorchester, I received orders to send a reinforcement immediately to that place."

"November 10, 1775. To Capt. Francis Marion: You are to proceed with all expedition, with yours and Capt. Huger's

FORT DORCHESTER

← 103 FT. →

SALLY PORT

Ashley River

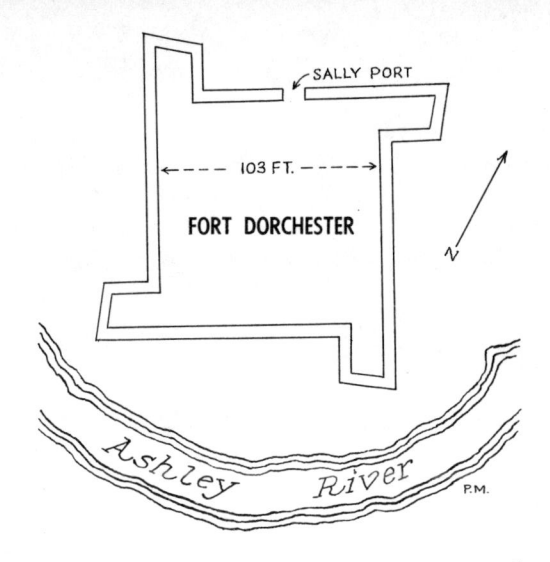

companies, to Dorchester to reinforce the troops there, and to take special care in guarding and defending the cannon, gunpowder and public records at that place. You are to take command of the whole forces there until further orders. You are to apply to the committee at Dorchester for sufficient numbers of Negroes in the public service to remove the cannon lying near the waterside to a spot more safe near the fort."

(signed "William Moultrie.")

In May 1778, General Moultrie formed his army at Dorchester. A year later, he stopped at Dorchester again to reform his troops before moving to Charleston to help defend that city. In February 1780, Sir Henry Clinton landed and the British began the seige against Charleston. April 13, 1780, British Cavalry under Tarleton marched up the Ashley River and captured Dorchester. The following month, Charleston fell. Dorchester became a British garrison. At the time of capture, Lt. Allaire, serving with Ferguson's Loyal Americans, described Dorchester as a small village with about 40 houses and a church.

On July 14, 1781, Colonel "Light Horse Harry" Lee and his troops reoccupied Dorchester and captured a good supply of horses and ammunition from the retreating British. The British returned, but were driven out for good on December 1, 1781, by General Nathanael Green and Col. Wade Hampton. The British did not wait for the attack to begin. During the night, they destroyed their supplies, threw their cannon into the river, and retreated with their 150 cavalry and 400 foot soldiers. From then on, Dorchester remained in American control.

81

After the Revolutionary War, Dorchester decayed rapidly. Only five years later, March, 1788, Bishop Asbury made the following entry in his journal: "I passed Dorchester where there are the remains of what appears to have been a once considerable town. There are ruins of an elegant church and the vestiges of several well built houses."

POSTAL SERVICE

When the first post office was established at Dorchester is unknown. According to records in the National Archives and Records Service in Washington, D. C., the first postmaster to send a report to the Postmaster General in Washington was William Harley, April 1, 1804. Then followed reports from William Creggmiles, July 1, 1805, and Richard Maynard, October 1, 1810. The dates of appointment as postmaster for these three were not given.

However, the exact dates of appointment is given for Henry Clayton, July 2, 1810; Edward Hughes, April 21, 1820; Benjamin Peter Simons, 1823, month and day not given; George M. Hughes, July 10, 1824; James L. Morris, May 9, 1826; and John R. Coburn, March 10, 1827.

The post office at Dorchester was closed on June 6, 1826. By this time the town was deserted.

DORCHESTER SLUMBERS

Dorchester died for the following reasons: (1) The migration between 1752-57 of all the Congregational Church members to Midway, Georgia. (2) The advance inland of the frontier which deprived Dorchester of its military and commercial importance as an outpost. (3) The extension of a network of good roads, and the improvement of river navigation which made dealing directly with Charleston possible. (4) The decline of rice as the leading money crop made Dorchester's swampy location unimportant. (5) It has been reported that malaria was a minor disease prior to the Revolutionary, but that more virulent strains followed the war making Dorchester a health hazard.

Today, nothing remains of this once thriving community but a few memories contained in a few musty records. There was no historian present during its lifetime to record the triumphs, the defeats, the joys and the sorrows of this vanished town.